MAKING

OF THE

WHITEMAN

History, Tradition and The
Teachings of Elijah Muhammad

Paul Lawrence Guthrie

Distributed By:

Lushena Books

607 Country Club Drive, Unit E
Bensenville, IL 60106
Tel: 630-238-8708
Fax: 630-238-8824
Email:Lushena@aol.com

Beacon Communications

Published By

BEACON COMMUNICATIONS
4951 Clairemont Square Suite 137
San Diego, CA 92117

Library of Congress Number : 98-67887

DEDICATED TO LOUIS FARRAKHAN AND THE NATION OF ISLAM.

CONTENTS

CHAPTER 1
What Is This Book All About? 1
An Overview of Ancient History 2

CHAPTER 2
History and the Teachings
of Elijah Muhammad 12
Traditional Accounts Used in the
Study of Ancient History 14
A Search For Similarities 15
Real History Symbolically Told 15

CHAPTER 3
Scholars Who Agree 29
Religion Acknowledges the
Existence of Men Before Adam 31

CHAPTER 4
Adam Represents a Group of People 36
Adam Made By a Group of People 36
Adam Means "Whiteman" 39

CHAPTER 5
Whiteman Driven From Civilization 42
Ancient Writings Agree With Muhammad 45
Preserved in the Shah-Nama 45
Recorded in the Writings of Diodorus 46
Facts Consistent With the Story of
Adam and Eve 49
The Book of Adam and Eve 49
Outlined in the History of the Jinn 52
Sent to the Caucasus Mountains 54
The Caucasian People 56
Re-enacted in the Atonement 59
In the Caves for 2,000 Years 61
Acknowledged by Tibetan Buddhists 63

CHAPTER 6
The Hills and Caves of West Asia 66
The Walls of the Caucasus 66
The Desert Bandits 71
Oral Traditions of the Caucasus Mountains 74
Life Inside the Caves 78
The Land of Mazandaran 81
Whites Referred to as Devils in
Ancient Egypt 85
Musa 89
Conclusion 93
References 94

CHAPTER 1

WHAT IS THIS BOOK ALL ABOUT?

This book examines a series of events that took place long ago in and around the region of the Near East. Those events include the disruption of civilization, the sudden arrival of white people in the vicinity of the Caucasus Mountains and what happened 2,000 years later when they unexpectedly came out of the hills and attacked the centers of civilization. By examining these events we will be able to better determine to what extent the facts of history agree with the teachings of Elijah Muhammad.

An understanding of the material offered in this book depends, in part, on the reader's familiarity with some of the more important trends that occurred in the history of the ancient world. Chapter 1 starts by offering an overview of those trends. In this way the first chapter is intended to re-familiarize the reader and to present him or her with an outline of the facts upon which the rest of this book is based. Afterwards we will begin to examine how all of these events relate to the teachings of Muhammad.

AN OVERVIEW OF ANCIENT HISTORY

Between six and seven thousand years ago, signs of disruption began to appear throughout the ancient civilizations of the Near East. For nearly a thousand years the cultures of that region underwent a change; a period of regression. The historical record shows that large groups of people moved into and out of the region. As chaos and dissatisfaction grew, problems intensified and the ancient societies of the Near East slipped deeper into despair. Then, about 6,000 years ago, the inevitable happened - civilization fell apart.[1]

What caused the breakup of civilization six thousand years ago? Many experts have tried to address this issue, but so far no clear explanation has been found. Some historians had speculated that a natural disaster, such as an earthquake or some similar event took place, but they were unable to find any evidence to support their claims. Besides, all of the clues pointed in the direction of an event quite different from that of an earthquake - a condition that grew over an extended period of time. The picture is one of communities in turmoil, of societies collapsing and falling apart from within; of chaos, dissatisfaction and unrest. The most accurate summation would be to say that the people just began fighting and killing one another - this is the best way to describe what was happening in the Near East 6,000 years ago.[2]

Soon after the unsettling of civilization, another interesting change began to take place. This change occurred in the area of the Caucasus Mountains. There, in West Asia, a previously unknown group of people suddenly appeared as if from out of nowhere. Collectively they are known as the Indo-Europeans, Caucasians or white people. The facts show that they first entered the area around 6,000 years ago. 2,000 years later their invasions would bring them into contact with the civilized nations to the south. But as to where they first came from and how they finally ended up living in West Asia, very little appears to be known. Because they had no fixed homes and wandered about from place to place, historians usually describe their way of life as 'nomadic'. In the book *A History of the Ancient World*, Chester Starr talks about their lack of culture and their uncivilized way of life. As for their language and the uncertainty surrounding their place of origin, Starr said of them:

"Since they were so backward, it is very difficult to use archaeological evidence to help pin down the original home of the Indo-European tongues. No specific patterns of physical culture can be attached to the languages; and they were written only after their speakers came into contact with civilized peoples."[3]

With the arrival of the Caucasians into that cold and sparsely populated area of the world, the few older communities, which earlier had been established there in Europe were either abandoned or destroyed. The evidence clearly suggests that the original inhabitants of those settlements either fled or were killed off by the newly arriving whites. In an article appearing in the *Journal of Indo-European Studies*, Professor Marija Gimbutas talked about the arrival of the whites and the subsequent disintegration of what she calls "Old Europe" - the farms and villages that had existed in Europe before the arrival of the whiteman. According to Gimbutas, after the whites showed up, drastic changes started to occur in the region north of the Caucasus. Explaining how those changes signalled the arrival of the Caucasians, Gimbutas says:

"A time period around 3500 B.C. forms a *caesura* between Old Europe and Indo-European Europe. It is a time when life in the large villages and townships either stops or is markedly changed. It is at this time - the first half of the fourth millennium B.C. - that the first eruption into the Danubian and northern European plains of the Kurgan or Proto-Indo-European peoples from the lower Volga lower Don steppe is dated (Gimbutas, 1970). The degenerative changes in the settlements of the Old European Civilization may be assumed to indicate the beginning of the Indo-European presence."[4]

Following the breakup of the ancient societies and the arrival of the whiteman in Europe, the people of the Near East worked to re-establish the level of peace and security they had once known. Slowly, over time, communities were rebuilt, prosperity was restored and signs of the new life started to emerge.

In Africa, along the banks of the Nile River, Egypt blossomed into the Pyramid Age. In Mesopotamia, between the Tigris and Euphrates Rivers, the Sumerians too, established a civilization renown for its high level of culture and refinement. Even as far away as India, along the tributaries of the Indus River, the Dravidians constructed the magnificent twin cities of Mohenjo-Daro and Harrapa. Rich in arts, sciences and the necessities of life these civilizations laid the foundations for trade and finance, architecture, geometry, mathematics and astronomy, philosophy, law and government, writing and religion.

Throughout the period of reconstruction, not much attention was being paid to the nomads of the north; the threat never seemed significant. From time to time, a few nomadic bands would wander down into the centers of civilization, but their activities never amounted to more than occasional raids or skirmishes. In the course of time small groups of the whites were able to establish camps along the hills and deserts outside of Mesopotamia. Although such camps survived mainly by robbing and scavenging, their overall impact upon civilization remained minimal; most of the whites were at that time still beyond range, up in the hills.

In the book *The Chalice and the Blade*, Riane Eisler, the internationally known scholar, talks about the distant presence of the whites and the low level of concern that their activities invoked. On page 43 Eisler explains:

"At first it was like the proverbial biblical cloud "no bigger than a man's hand" - the activities of seemingly insignificant nomadic bands roaming the less desirable fringe areas of our globe....Over millennia they were apparently out there in the harsh, unwanted, colder, sparser territories on the edge of the earth, while the first great agricultural civilizations spread out along the lakes and rivers in the fertile heartlands. To these agricultural peoples, enjoying humanity's early peak of evolution, peace and prosperity must have seemed the blessed eternal state for humankind, the nomads no more than a peripheral novelty."[5]

But the Caucasians of the north were not to remain a distant novelty forever. 2,000 years after their arrival, the nomadic tribes began to move away from what for years had been their home. As they swarmed down, out of the hills, some of them began to travel west, toward the Aegean Sea. At the same time another large group trudged southward, in the direction of the centers of civilization. The unforeseen mass movement of white people out of the hills of West Asia has generally been looked upon as a historical mystery. That is why most historians agree with Chester Starr who in his attempt to explain it, characterized the whiteman's unexpected awakening this way: "*...for unknown reasons*, the group went into a ferment shortly before 2000 BC. and started spilling out all over europe and western Asia."[6]

As they moved southward, they were joined by smaller groups - members of their own who had earlier taken up positions along the hills and caravan routes outside of Mesopotamia. As they advanced toward the centers of civilization, they began a series of violent and devastating attacks. One by one the great cities of the ancient world began to topple. So complete was the effect of the onslaught that when it was all over, nothing was left standing. In the book *A World History*, William Hardy MacNeill outlined what took place. On page 43, Professor Mac Neill tells us:

"During a period of about three hundred years, beginning soon after 1700 B.C., the civilized world was overrun by barbarian conquerors. Hill peoples living north and east of Mesopotamia, tribesmen from the desert fringes of Syria, Palestine, and northern Arabia, together with wide ranging war bands originating from the northern steppe combined in varying proportions to attack all existing centers of civilized life. The range of these barbarian conquests was never again equaled....At the two extremes of the civilized world, in Crete and in India, little but smoking ruins remained..."[7]

So the facts show that after the reconstruction of civilization, the whites came out of the hills and destroyed it all. The devastation that rocked the ancient world occurred across the board. It is for this reason that, if we look at the early history of Civilization, we find that *all* of the centers of civilization, throughout the Near East, Africa, Mesopotamia and India underwent a severe fall at about the same period of time. Every historian agrees that the uprooting of those civilizations were the result of attacks from white barbarians who came rushing down, out of the hills of West Asia.

In India, Mohenjo-daro was sacked and its people were enslaved or killed. The outcome was the same for those of Mesopotamia and Egypt too. The extent to which the nomadic tribes overran and subjugated civilization is echoed in the writings of Immanuel Velikovsky who described what the whites did in

Egypt by saying: "A cruel conqueror invaded the once mighty realm, now overthrown and prostrate he subjugated it without meeting resistance; he desecrated its sacred places; he raped its surviving women, enslaved the decimated population. He utterly destroyed the temples, if any remained erect, robbed the sepulchers of the dead, and ,mutilated the victims who remained alive."[8]

Ancient accounts, some of which were written by the Egyptians themselves, clearly illustrate the gloom into which the ancient societies had fallen. Such eye-witness accounts demonstrate how the whiteman came in and violently usurped the ancient cultures by turning the wealth and sophistication of those civilizations into his own. One such document, *The Admonitions of Ipu-Wer*, was written in Egypt right after the whiteman had gained control over the land. The account describes the invading nomads as crude and cultureless barbarians who forced their way into Egypt, beatup the population and then stripped the original inhabitants of their possessions. Regarding these matters, *The Admonitions of Ipu-Wer* reads:

"Barbarians from outside have come to Egypt.... the children of nobles are dashed against the walls....The storehouse is stripped bare; its keeper is stretched out on the ground....Behold now, something has been done which has never happened

....he who never even slept on a plank is now the owner of a bed....Behold, the owners of robes are now in rags. But he who never wove for himself is now the owner of fine linen....Behold, she who once looked at her face in the water is now the owner of a mirror."[9]

In Sumeria, the facts present a similar picture. Fragments from one Sumerian account tell of the destruction of the city of Ur, and reads in part: "..the population laments bitterly...the catastrophe which has overtaken the city...the city lies in ruins."[10]

In India, the conquering horde, known as the Aryans, came down from the hills and pillaged the peaceful farming communities of northern India. *Indian Gods and Kings*, by E. Hawkridge tells all about what happened. On page 10, Hawkridge explains: "...at the northwest corner...there was a break in the mountain wall....Down upon the Dravidians farming in the north came sudden surprising attacks from ruddy tribes."[11]

Through the streets of Mohenjo-daro the whiteman ran wild - robbing, raping and slaughtering who dared to stand in his way. Modern Archaeologists have uncovered evidence which shows that in Mohenjo-daro even the women and children were beaten to death. As historian H.G. Rawlinson pointed out: "Mohenjo-daro was sacked and its inhabitants put to the sword. Groups of skeletons, including women and children, have been found, some in a large room, others at the foot of a staircase leading down to a well, and others again in a street. Their contorted attitudes suggest that they met a violent death."[12]

For all practical purposes the arrival of the whiteman signalled the end of civilization as it once existed. Along with the invasions came a new style of life. In India the Aryans set up a social order based on skin color, called the caste system. According to that system, the whites were the rulers and the darker-skinned Dravidians turned into slaves and outcastes. In Egypt and Mesopotamia the priests were turned into slaves and the other dark-skinned persons were relegated to menial positions or were pushed back away from the areas of trade and commerce. The new way of life was drastically different from anything that had existed before - it was the beginning of the whiteman's rise to power.

CHAPTER 2

HISTORY AND THE TEACHINGS OF ELIJAH MUHAMMAD

The disruption of the ancient civilizations of the Near East, the sudden arrival of white people in the vicinity of the Caucasus Mountains and what took place 2,000 years later when they rushed out of the hills and invaded civilization are among the historical events presented in the teachings of Elijah Muhammad.

One of the significant features of Muhammad's teachings is his bold and unique approach when it comes to clarifying some of the unexplainable aspects of these events. For instance, Elijah Muhammad says that 6,000 years ago a new race of people showed up in the region of the Near East. The new race, Muhammad says, were white people. He says that the whites first appeared 6,000 years ago on the Island of Pelan, in the Aegean Sea, where they had been "made" by a process of selective breeding called "grafting". According to Muhammad, it was black people, living on the Island of Pelan who gave birth to the whites. Under their leader, Yakub, the blacks of Pelan were placed under a system of laws by which marriage was based on skin color and in which only lighter complexioned babies were allowed to survive. Muhammad teaches that over the course of many generations, the population of Pelan began to grow lighter and lighter until, after 600 years of *grafting*, the people had become very pale and white.

When some of the whites from Pelan showed up in the Near East, their presence created a calamity. As a result they were driven out, away from the people and into the hills of West Asia. There, Muhammad teaches, they remained for the next 2,000 years.

Following the driving away of the whites, they became isolated and cut off; without proper guidance and the things to start a civilization of their own and, as a result, Elijah Muhammad explains, they slipped into a life of savagery. He says that 2,000 years later and usurped civilization from the original people . [13]

Since history shows that a disruption had occurred in the Near East just prior to the sudden appearance of the white people in the hills of West Asia is it possible that the teachings of Elijah Muhammad are indeed rooted in fact? Inasmuch as no other reasonable explanation has been presented to explain these occurrences, and since the evidence is consistent with what Muhammad says took place, is it reasonable to suggest that what Muhammad teaches is in fact true?

TRADITIONAL ACCOUNTS USED IN THE STUDY OF ANCIENT HISTORY

What are traditional accounts and how are they used in the study of ancient history? Traditional Accounts are stories or narratives that in ancient times had been used to explain important historical events and which were passed down from one generation to another. Up until the turn of the century, traditional accounts were often viewed as meaningless tales without any real historical value, but today historians recognize that such accounts can be very helpful in bettering our understanding of the past. Modernly, traditional accounts often help explain the manners and customs of the people, as well as the time and place in which they originated. The use of ancient traditional accounts in the study of history has even led to some surprising discoveries.

A clear example of this occurred in the case of Heinrich Schliemann, the famous archaeologist who in 1876 carried a copy of *The Iliad* along during his search for the Lost City of Troy. Troy, an ancient city in Turkey, had long been popularized in *The Iliad*, a collection of Greek myths and legends. Schliemann, believed that the information contained in those myths, would guide him to the exact location of the lost city.

Schliemann's search led him to a hill, 4 miles from the Dardanelles and which seemed to fit the geographical location of Troy described in *The Iliad.* Convinced that the city lay buried beneath the hill, Schliemann began to dig and before long he unearthed what has since been called the greatest archaeological discovery of the 19th century. From the hole he had dug, Schliemann uncovered the remains of Troy, including many pounds of gold jewelry and an assortment of other valuable artifacts. The re-discovery of Troy laid the foundation upon which all later studies of ancient Greece were to be based. Heinrich Schliemann's re-discovery allowed many historians to increase their understanding of the past. It was an achievement made possible through the use of ancient traditional accounts.[14]

A SEARCH FOR SIMILARITIES

Ancient narratives that purport to describe a series of actual events are historically useful when it can be shown that they point to *real* places and events. Whether they do or not is determined by the number of similarities that exist between the words of the account and the actual places or events themselves. The most popularly known traditional account which shares similarities with the teachings of Elijah Muhammad is the Bible's story of Adam and Eve. According to the Old Testament, Adam was made 6,000 years ago. (This date is arrived at by adding together the ages of all of the Patriarchs from Adam to Abraham as they appear in the 5th and 11th chapters of the book of Genesis.)[15] Accordingly, the time of Adam's "creation" corresponds with the time which Muhammad says white people first appeared on the planet. In addition, the Bible's record of the making and subsequent driving away of Adam and Eve from the Garden, fits perfectly into the time frame established for the sudden arrival of the Caucasians in the hills of West Asia. In his book, *Message to the Blackman*, Elijah Muhammad explains that the Bible's account of Adam and Eve is in actuality a narrative of the early history of the Caucasian race.[16]Could the story of Adam and Eve be an accounting of the early history of the Caucasian people? What are the facts in this regard? A review of the traditions of the making of Man as they exist around the world shows a surprising number of them to be in full agreement with Muhammad - they relate that Adam and Eve had white complexions. Some depict the new made-man as starting out with a darker complexion, and then later being transformed to white.

One such account has been handed down in the traditions of the Maidu Indians. In their record of the making of Man, the Maidu point out that in the beginning, God made two people out of dark red clay, but that one day after a garden was planted those same two people turned very white. Not only is the Maidu account similar to the Bible's story of Adam and Eve, but it also offers information supportive of the position that the first white people were somehow transformed out of an earlier darker-skinned people.

In his book *Folk-Lore in the Old Testament*, George G. Frazer quotes from the Maidu account. Regarding God's making of Man as preserved in Maidu tradition, Frazer writes: "One day he took dark red earth, mixed it with water, and fashioned two figures, one of them a man and the other a woman..." The next morning, he "thrust a piece of pitch-wood into the ground, and fire burst out. The two people were very white. No one today is so white as they were."[17]

A similar tradition, from India, explains that the first Caucasians were made when a group of dark-skinned people gave birth to light complexioned babies who in turn gave birth to a nation of albinos from whom other whites were born. Dr. John Davy, mentions this tradition and considers the possibility of the white race having originated in this manner in his book, *Account of the Island of Ceylon*. As to the likelihood that whites first came into existence through a means similar to this, Dr. Davy admitted: "It is easy to conceive that an accidental variety of the kind might propagate, and that the White race of mankind is sprung from such an accidental variety. The East Indians are of this opinion; and there is a tradition or story among them in which this origin is assigned to us."[18]

The views of scientists, like Dr. Davy and others, concerning the origin of the white race generally are in accord with Muhammad's teachings in that most agree that white people had to have come into being by way of darker-skinned parents. This much, at least, was admitted by L. Bolk who in an article entitled *Origin of Racial Characteristics in Man*, wrote: "White skin...started from an ancestor with a black skin, in whose offspring hair and iris color were suppressed more and more."[19] That description matches perfectly with what Elijah Muhammad refers to as grafting.

When Charles Darwin discussed the origins of race he too expressed the opinion that selection, over the course of many generations, had to have been used in bringing about what he called "the characteristic differences between the races of man." He even went on to concluded that without some form of selective breeding, such racial differences simply "cannot be accounted for in a satisfactory manner."[20] Darwin's findings that new races were formed by continuing to marry offspring who shared similar physical characteristics is consistent with Muhammad's explanation of the grafting process.[21] James Cowles Prichard, the British Anthropologist looked at the facts and concluded that the physical differences between the races of Man could only have resulted from a method comparable to "the process of artificial selection carried on by plant and animal breeders."[22] This too is consistent with the words of Elijah Muhammad.

When it came to answering the question of where all of this selective breeding could have taken place, Dr. Edwin Grant Conklin, a Professor of Biology at Princeton University pointed out that "geographic isolation," similar to the kind that Muhammad said occurred on the Island of Pelan, definitely played a role in the formative stages of the races. In his book, *The Evolution of Man*, Dr. Conklin wrote: "...it is evident that distinct races could not have been established and perpetuated except by the aid of isolation, chiefly geographical."[23]

What does all of this mean? Only that experts agree that some form of grafting had to have taken place. However, they have been unable to indentify exactly where it took place or who was in charge of it.

Thus, it is with good reason that when asked whether a new race could be produced by separating specific individuals who possess similar genetic traits and selectively breeding or grafting them over the course of several generations, as taught by Elijah Muhammad, the experts have to agree with Dr. Ramm who admitted: "By scientific breeding we can shuffle these genes with their characteristics, and breed traits in or breed them out....The laws of heredity plus principles of separation or selection operating over a period of time will produce the various races of the world."[24]

So Elijah Muhammad's teaching that the white race came into being as a result of a form of selective breeding is not at all unreasonable. That is why it was so easy for Dr.Davy to consider the earlier East Indian tradition that described the birth of white people from dark-skinned parents.

Another ancient traditional account that shares similarities with the teachings of Muhammad is the biblical account of Jacob's grafted flock. Genesis 30:35 says that Jacob (the english translation of the name Yakub) was able to produce unusually colored flocks of sheep and goat through the use of a skillful breeding technique. According to the Bible, it took Jacob six years to successfully change the color of the flock (Genesis:31:41).

That the Bible's story of Jacob's grafted flock is related to the birth of white people from Black parents is attested to by the ancient book of Jewish traditions called the *Midrash Rabbah*. There a discussion is recorded between the Black king of Arabia and the Jewish scholar, Akiba. In that discussion, the Black king is said to have stated:

"I am a black and my wife is a black, yet she gave birth to a white son."

To which, Akiba's response was:

"If you are surprised at such a possibility, study the case of our father Jacob's flock, which were influenced in their conception by the rods."[25]

In Akiba's response he drew a connection between the birth of a white-skinned child to black parents with the case of Jacob's (or Yakub's) grafting of an unusually colored flock. That it took Jacob six years to graft his flock parallels with Muhammad's history of Yakub. Moreover, the name *Akiba*,like Jacob is also a variant of the name "Yakub."

So the idea that whites originated from Black people is by no means a new idea. In an article entitled *Metallurgical Anthropology in Hesiod and Plato*," Robert Eisler traces the origins of the 4 ages back to the teachings of the Black Nubians and their allies, the Phoenicians. Eisler reports that during the time of Black Nubian rule in Egypt, the Phoenicians were busy circulating a call to all pale-skinned nations, demanding that they lay down their arms and submit to the rule of the Blacks. According to Eisler, the Blacks then were of the view that the pale-skinned whites "represented successive stages of degeneration from the aboriginal perfection of the Nubian golden race".[26]

This again is simply another way of saying that the original people were Black and that all other races came from that original group. As Eisler also correctly pointed out, this is also the real meaning behind the greek stories which speak of "The Golden Age".

Writing toward the end of the period historians call the Greek Dark Age-the three or four hundred years following the Dorian invasions-the ancient poet Hesiod acknowledges that there once was a "golden race." "All good things," Hesiod writes, "were theirs. The Fruitful earth poured forth her fruits unbidden in boundless plenty. In peaceful ease they kept their lands with good abundance, rich in flocks and dear to the immortals."[27] The golden race were the blacks and the golden age was the period before the arrival of the whiteman.

In *The Chalice and the Blade, Eisler states* : "An earlier time when humans led more harmonius lives is also a recurrent theme in the legends of Mesopotamia. Here there are repeated references to a time of plenty and peace, a time before a great flood, when women and men lived in an idyllic garden. These are the stories from which biblical scholars now believe the Old Testament myth of the Garden of Eden in part derives."[28] Hinting that the story of Adam and Eve actually outlines of the disruption of civilization, Eisler went on to write: "Likewise, the Garden of Eden and Fall from Paradise myths in part draw from actual historical events....these stories reflect the cataclysmic cultural change...the imposition of male dominance and the accompanying shift from peace and partnership to dominance and strife."[29] This we now know talks about the arrival of the whiteman.

What does all of this mean? Only that the facts of history are consistent with the teachings of Elijah Muhammad and that those teachings are also supported by the findings of Anthropologists as well as by numerous traditional accounts from various parts of the world.

REAL HISTORY SYMBOLICALLY TOLD

Many of the traditions of the ancient Near East tell of events and circumstances identical in every way to those taught by Elijah Muhammad. Viewed individually, it is easy to attribute such similarities to coincidence, but when collectively examined the ancient accounts present a pattern so overwhelmingly consistent with the teachings of Muhammad that they leave no doubt as to the certainty of their meaning.

A number of accounts are included in this category. Each tell of the birth of a white-skinned child whose arrival signals the beginning of trouble and chaos and who ends up being driven away from the people and taken to a remote location high in the Caucasus Mountains. Historically, such accounts narrate the birth and arrival of a new race of people; the disruptions which followed and the driving away of that new race into the hills of West Asia.

Such are the details that appear in the history of ancient Persia. The history of ancient Persia is outlined in its national epic, called the *Shah-Nama*. This ancient account relates an event in which two dark-skinned parents give birth to a white-skinned son. The boy's father was terrified by the unusual color of the child and he immediately announced to the people that his newly arrived son belonged to "a race of devils". Soon thereafter, a group of men from among the elders of the city issue a warning concerning the white child's future. Turning toward the father of the boy, the elders declare:"This will be to thee productive of nothing but calamity."[30]

As in the story of Adam and Eve, a decision was made to remove the child (Adam) from the region. In the words of the *Shah-Nama* the white-skinned boy was then stripped bare and "removed from the land and abandoned in some remote place...far from association with man."[31] Thus the child was siezed and taken to Mount Alburz, in the heart of the Caucasus Mountains. There the boy was abandoned. Isolated and alone he grew up naked and without shelter.

Another tradition, recorded in *The Book of Enoch*, also fits this familiar pattern and states that Lamech's wife gave birth to a white-skinned son. Lamech's white-skinned son likewise ends up in the Caucasus Mountains - on Mount Ararat. According to the version found in *The Book of Enoch*, Lamech, the boy's father, described the child as "changed", "unlike" and "of a different nature" than those who had lived before him. As in the other accounts the newly arrived child's skin is said to have been "white as snow" and his hair was blonde. *The Book of Enoch* talks about what happened when

Lamech learned that his wife had given birth to the uncommonly colored child. In this regard, chapter 105 states:

"She became pregnant by him, and brought forth a child, the flesh of which was white as snow and red as a rose; the hair of whose head was white...and long....Lamech his father was afraid of him; and flying away to his own father Methusalah, said: I have begotten a son, a changed son. He is not human; but...is of a different nature from ours, being altogether unlike to us."[32]

Here the circumstances surrounding the birth of the white-skinned child symbolically represent the arrival, of a new white-skinned race of people into the region of the Near East.

Lamech's father,Methusalah, not knowing what to make of the unusual-looking boy, went seeking the advice of his own father, Enoch. Thus Methusalah went to Enoch and said:

"...a child has been born...whose nature is not like the nature of man. His color is whiter than the snow; he is redder than the rose; the hair of his head is whiter than white...And behold I am come to thee, that thou mightest point out to me the truth."[33]

Methusalah's last statement suggests there to be a hidden meaning or symbolic purpose associated with the birth of the child; that the child's birth is only an allegory signalling the beginning of some important historical event. Enoch's response to Methusalah's shocking announcement confirms that a change was in fact about to occur. Following Methusalah's announcement Enoch responds: "Then I Enoch, answered and said: The lord will effect a new thing upon the earth."[34]

So the words "a new thing upon the earth" forewarn that a change was about to take place, following the arrival of the white-skinned child. Moreover, Enoch's words indicate that the arrival of the child would bring about a change that would affect the whole earth; that it would alter the course of civilization. This is much the same as what Elijah Muhammad says happened in the Near East 6,000 years ago - and the facts bear him out.

In the bible, a similar change occurs following the arrival of Adam and his subsequent expulsion from the Garden. *The Holy Qu'ran* also says that just before the making of Adam, the angels warned that Adam's arrival would only "create mischief and cause the shedding of blood."[35] The nature of that warning is similar in many ways to the one issued by the elders in *the Shah-Nama* and the prophetic words of Methusalah to Enoch. In each example, the phrases "calamity", "a new thing", "mischief" and "the shedding of blood" accurately describe the disturbance that swept through the ancient societies of the Near East and upset the course of civilization 6,000 years ago. Are these accounts really historical narratives of events that occurred long ago. Let's take a closer look at some of the accounts, beginning with the Bible's story of Adam and Eve.

CHAPTER 3

SCHOLARS WHO AGREE

An objection might be raised that the Book of Genesis has nothing whatsoever to do with the arrival of white people into the Near East, and that instead the story of Adam and Eve only talks about the making of the first man and woman. This objection, while no doubt a popular one, goes against the evidence and is inconsistent with the findings of all those who have considered the facts.

Throughout the years many people have stepped forward to comment on the true meaning of the Genesis account. Of those who have written on the subject, a great majority of them agree with Elijah Muhammad - that the making of Adam represents the birth of white people and that dark-skinned people existed before the making of Adam.

One such writer, Dr. C.W. Shields, devoted many years of research to this field of study and concluded that the story of Adam and Eve narrates the birth of the first Caucasians. Throughout his writings, Shields also acknowledges that the human family did not start with Adam. In his book, *The Scientific Evidences of Revealed Religion*, C.W. Shields wrote: "The Genesis record, deals with the Adamite-Caucasian race...although the human race is wider than the scope of the Caucasians and much earlier than the Adamites."[36]

Other scholars have expressed similar points of view. In his book, *The Genesis of the Earth and of Man*, Reginald Stuart Poole, of the British Museum, also surveyed the facts and found that both science and the bible teach the existence of Man before the making of Adam. In addition, Dr. Poole found that Adam was only "the first individual of a new variety of a species." Regarding the racial significance of his findings, Poole admitted that "Adam was the progenitor of the white race only; and that before the creation of Adam, the Black Race had been established in the continent of Africa."[37]

Dr. J.P. Thompson, another scientist, also concluded that the bible's story of Adam and Eve outlines the early history of the caucasian race. One of his books, *Man in Genesis and Geology*, characterizes this view as "one possible way in which the Bible and Science may yet be harmonized..."[38]

These are just a few of the many scholars who have examined the facts. Their studies have led them to adopt positions which agree with the teachings of Elijah Muhammad. In their writings they have concluded that the bible's story of Adam and Eve relates to the arrival of the world's first white people; they agree that dark-skinned people did not come from Adam but instead were already in existence at the time when Adam was made.

RELIGION ACKNOWLEDGES THE EXISTENCE OF MEN BEFORE ADAM

Elijah Muhammad teaches that the early history of the white race is set forth in the bible's account of Adam and Eve. In this regard, he teaches that Adam represents a group of people - white people - and that they were made or first came into existence through black people. In addition, Mr. Muhammad says that much of what he teaches in this regard has been known among scholars for a very long time and that a study of the facts would affirm his claim.

One clear example that verifies the accuracy of Elijah Muhammad's position is found in the case of Tomas Scoto, the fourteenth century Spanish monk who was put on trial and executed after he tried to reveal information identical to that taught by Elijah Muhammad. Tomas Scoto said that the story of Adam and Eve simply told of the making of one group of people by another. Records kept by the Church of Spain show that Tomas Scoto was charged with the crime of spreading an "unauthorized" view of the scriptures. At his trial, the monk responded to the charges against him by declaring in latin: "Ante Adam fuerunt homines et per illos homines fuit factus Adam", meaning: "There were men before Adam and Adam was made by those men."[39] Tomas Scoto endured great suffering on behalf of this belief. How closely do his words compare with the teachings of Elijah Muhammad?

Although some may choose to believe that the human family started with Adam, the Bible itself never says that Adam was the first man. Instead, the bible is in total harmony with the facts of science, all of which show that the history of Man goes back well beyond 6,000 years. Leon Poliakov hinted in this direction when in his book, *The Aryan Myth,* he suggested: "Long before the Christian era, some of the older Jewish exegetes concluded, from certain passages in the Book of Genesis, that the universe might have had an earlier creation and that part of this might have continued to exist - angels, demons or men perhaps better, perhaps worse than the posterity of Adam."[40]

A similar view existed among early Muslim scholars as well. During the tenth century, the Muslim historian al-Masudi taught that not all men were descended from Adam. To help demonstrate his position, al-Masudi produced a list of 28 nations - all of whom, he demonstrated, had existed from before the time of Adam.[41]

In the same century, another Muslim scholar, al-Maqdisi is known to have reached the same conclusion. Al-Maqdisi cited verses from *The Holy Qur'an* as authority for his statements. Quoting chapter 2, verse 28, al-Maqdisi showed where the angels had accused Adam of being a murderer. According to al-Maqdisi, the people who Adam murdered were those who had already been living on the earth prior to his arrival.[42]

Knowledge of the fact that people lived on the earth before the time of Adam is found among the early followers of Jesus as well - this claim is confirmed in the writings of the early Church Fathers, most notably St. Paul and St. Augustine.

In the year 1655, Isaac de La Peyrere, a sagacious priest of the orthodox faith, upset christian authorities by publishing a book called *Men Before Adam*. In that book, de La Peyrere showed how verses from the New Testament teach that Adam was not the first man and that people had lived before the time of Adam. Quoting from the Epistles of St. Paul, Peyrere had set out to establish two things: first, that the New Testament teaches the existence of men before Adam; and secondly, that the early followers of Jesus viewed Adam as "the first man" only in the sense that he was " the first man a sinner."[43]

The main points of Isaac de La Peyrere's position were based on three verses from the *Book of Romans*. Those verses read:

"Wherefore, as by one man sin entered into the world, and death by sin; and so death passed upon all men, for that all have sinned:

"For until the law sin was in the world: but sin is not imputed when there is no law.

"Nevertheless death reigned from Adam to Moses, even over them that had not sinned after the similitude of Adam's transgression, who is the figure of him that was to come."[44]

In his discussion, de La Peyrere first established the premise that the "one man" through whom "sin entered into the world" was Adam. He also noted that the sin, spoken of is the same one referred to as "Adam's transgression". From there, Peyrere reasoned, that since transgression is a violation of law, then "the law" here must be the one given to Adam. And since the phrase "until the law", implies a time before the law, then these verses must be saying that sin was in the world before the making of Adam - therefore, de La Peyrere concluded, people had to have been in existence before Adam in order for them to have committed that sin.

Isaac de La Peyrere's solution to these verses immediately captured the attention of the enlightened and free-thinkers of his day. But in the eyes of the Church, de La Peyrere was viewed an enemy and copies of his book were collected and publicly burned in Paris.[45]

All of the above examples should make it plain that what Elijah Muhammad teaches regarding the meaning of Adam and Eve is not just some new or made-up idea, but instead it is an idea that has been recognized among religious scholars from many different faiths and from as far back as we can remember.

But what about the actual words used in the bible's account of the making of Adam and Eve? Do the words of that account also agree with what has been taught by Muhammad?

CHAPTER 4

ADAM REPRESENTS A GROUP OF PEOPLE

Many of the Hebrew scholars have insisted that the name "Adam" (ADham) is a plural noun.[46] They mean by this, that it represents a group and not a singular individual. Moreover, that Adam is intended to represent a group of men and women is made clear by the way in which the name is used throughout the Old Testament. Among several examples are those that appear in *Genesis 1:27* and *Genesis 5:2*, both of which state:

"Male and Female created he them...and called their name Adam."[47]

Here, the Bible says that Adam is a group of men and women. If Adam were a single individual then the bible would not refer to him as "them". Certainly a group is being spoken of - but which group of men and women is Adam presumed to represent? Also, Who made Adam? And, What does the name "Adam" really mean?

ADAM MADE BY A GROUP OF PEOPLE

The Book of Genesis first speaks of the making

of Adam in the 26th verse of the 1st chapter. There, the words of the Old Testament describe Adam as a group of people who were about to be "made" by another group of people:

"And God said, Let us make man in our image, after our likeness: and let them have dominion over the fish of the sea,- and over the fowl of the air, and over the cattle, and over all the earth, and over every creeping thing that creepeth upon the earth."[48]

In this case the Bible not only calls Adam "them", but it also refers to the makers of Adam as "us". This shows that Adam and the Makers of Adam were in fact two separate groups of people. The english word "God", as it appears in this verse is a translation from the Hebrew word *Elohim*.[49] Like *Adam*, Elohim is also a plural noun - it indicates a group of beings and it too is both masculine and feminine.

G. de Purucker, chairman of the Theosophical Society, lectured on the significance of the word "Elohim" in a book called *Fundamentals of the Esoteric Philosophy*. Concerning the actual meaning of the word and how it refers to a plurality of beings, de Purucker pointed out: "The first part of it alone is EL, meaning GOD, divinity, from which comes the second, a feminine form, ELOH, GODDESS; IM is merely the masculine plural. So, if we translate every element in this single word it would mean, "god, goddess, plural."[50]

That the "gods and goddesses" whom the Bible credits with having made Adam were only a group of men and women can be plainly demonstrated by examining the way in which *Elohim* is used in other places throughout the bible. A survey of the facts reveals that *Elohim* is not actually a name but is instead only a title - one that in ancient times had been given to people who had distinguished themselves through some act or service. This much is even acknowledged in *The International Standard Bible Encyclopaedia*, which defines *Elohim* as a title designating "a position of honor and authority among men."[51]

One example that demonstrates how the word *Elohim* is used as a title of honor and authority among men is found in the Book of Exodus, where God informs Moses that he had been given authority higher than that of Pharaoh's: "And the Lord said unto Moses, See, I have made thee a god *(one of the Elohim)* to Pharaoh: and Aaron they brother shall be thy prophet."[52]

Biblical scholar, T. Rees, says that *Elohim* is just "a general term expressing majesty and authority."[53]

Lastly, R.A. Finlayson, Professor of Systematic Theology, wrote an article in which he plainly showed that the word Elohim "derives from a root indicating strength or might, and with this connotation," he wrote, "it is applied in the Old Testament to men."[54]Based on all of these facts it is evident that the Elohim were only a group of people.

ADAM MEANS 'WHITEMAN'

What is the real meaning of the name "Adam"? Many believe that Adam just means "Man" or "Mankind". But, the usual words for Man in the semitic languages generally are not cognate with the name Adam. Instead, the facts show that the name springs from the hebrew root 'dm, meaning "reddish in color"; concerning which, James Hastings writing in *The Encyclopaedia of Religion and Ethics*, adds: "the name having originated in a ruddy race."[55]

By the word ruddy is meant what the dictionary says of it, *pink colored* or *reddish*. This is what the name Adam actually means. Saying that Adam comes from a ruddy race is, as *The American College Dictionary* points out, the same as saying he was "pink or pinkish-red in color." The words "blushed" and "rosy-cheeked" are also synonymous with "ruddy".[56]

Descriptions of the whiteman as "red" or pink-colored appear all over the world. In addition, many of the older cultures are familiar with traditions which speak of the making of a pink or reddish colored man. In the book *Ethnic Pigmentation*, H. P. Wassermann notes in this regard: "The Bantu creation myth described (Adam and Eve) as red, which is the most accurate description for 'white people' and quite common in early descriptions of skin colour by dark races. 'Phoenician' means red skin, Russians with their rusty hair were originally 'Rustians', and 'Batuli', the north-Nigerian word for whites, also means 'redskin'."[57]

It is only reasonable to conclude that Adam's ruddy complexion was due to the lack of melanin in his skin. Because Adam's skin was pale it allowed the blood beneath to show through. Thus he appeared ruddy or pinkish-red in color. Regarding Adam's european characteristics as recorded by the early Hebrews, Alexander Winchell acknowledges: "...here is the old record which also declares that Adam was ruddy. This tint is found only in the Mediterranean race. The unmixed black races do not possess ruddy complexions." In conclusion, Winchell writes: "The ruddiness of Adam was...a complexion characteristically white."[58]

The Hebrew and English Lexicon also admits that Adam's name reveals the paleness of his complexion. In an article discussing the ruddy characteristics of Adam's skin, Dr. William Gesenius writes: "The Arabs distinguish two races of men: one red, ruddy, which we call white; the other black."[59]

So in Hebrew the name Adam is a plural noun. Scholars agree that it is a name used to describe a group of men and women. "Adam" means "pinkish-red" and the record indicates that it describes the characteristics of white people.

Since the facts show that Adam was a group of people and inasmuch as that group was white, then it only stands to reason that the bible's story of Adam and Eve concerns itself with the making of the whiteman as taught by Elijah Muhammad.

CHAPTER 5

WHITEMAN DRIVEN FROM CIVILIZATION

Six thousand years ago a change occurred in the civilizations of the Near East. The facts show that the cultures of that region underwent a change; a period of regression. At about the same time, white people suddenly appeared in West Asia, in the area of the Caucasus Mountains. In the teachings of Elijah Muhammad it is implied that both of these events are related. In his writings, Muhammad speaks of a disruption that swept through the region of the Near East and which was the result of dissatisfaction. In addition, he says the arrival of a new race (white people) led to additional problems. According to Muhammad, the circumstances surrounding the presence of the whites were such that soon it became necessary to remove them from among the people. So the Caucasians were driven away, across the desert. Finally, Muhammad teaches, they ended up in the hills and caves of West Asia. There they remained for the next 2,000 years.[60]

Mr. Muhammad outlines all of these events in his book *Message to the Blackman*. As to the disruption or calamity brought upon by the whites during that time, Muhammad writes: "They made trouble for six months...deceiving the ancient original people who were holy. But, when they learned just who was causing the trouble they...cast the troublemakers out into the worst and poorest part of our planet earth."[61] Describing what the whites had done to cause such trouble, Muhammad explains: "They accused the righteous people causing them to fight and kill one another."[62]

So, arguments and discord broke out between the original people and before long they were fighting and killing one another. These events, as Muhammad states them, are consistent with the historical evidence presented in chapter 1.

As to how all of this led to the driving away of the whites, Muhammad writes: "The holy people were unable to understand just why they could not get along in peace with each other, until they took the matter to the King. The King told the holy people of the black nation that the trouble they were having was caused by the white devils in their midst, and that there would be no peace among them until they drove these white made devils from among them."[63]

But before the whiteman was driven away from civilization, the King gave instructions to the people, outlining the procedures they were to follow. According to Muhammad, the King said: "Gather every one of the devils up and strip them of our costume. Put an apron on them to hide their nakedness. Take all literature from them and take them by way of the desert....Don't allow one of them to turn back; and, if they are lucky enough to get across the Arabian Desert, let them go into the hills of West Asia,..."[64]

So the fomenters of trouble were rounded up; stripped of all clothing; made to wear an apron; driven across the desert and finally released into the hills of West Asia. To insure that they would not return, guards were placed along the hills bordering the frontiers of civilization. As Muhammad states: "Once there, they were roped in, to keep them out of Paradise. To make sure, the Muslims, who lived along the borders of East and West Asia, were ordered to patrol the border to keep Yakub's devils in West Asia (now called Europe), so that the original nation of black men could live in peace; and that the devils could be alone to themselves, to do as they pleased, as long as they didn't try crossing the East border."[65]

Thus, shut away, without proper guidance and the things to start a civilization of their own, the whites soon lost the knowledge of civilization and slipped into a condition of life comparable to that of the animals. They remained in this savage state for the next 2,000 years. As Muhammad states: "They were punished by being deprived of divine guidance, for 2,000 years which brought them almost into the family of wild beasts - going upon all fours; eating raw and unseasoned, uncooked food; living in caves and treetops, climbing and jumping from one tree to the other."[66] What are the facts in this regard?

ANCIENT WRITINGS AGREE WITH MUHAMMAD

The presence of the Caucasians in the region of the Near East, the disruption caused by their presence and the way in which they were rounded up and driven away from the people is reflected in many of the writings of the ancient world.

PRESERVED IN THE SHAH-NAMA

Chapter 1 introduced a number of traditional accounts of the ancient world. One of those accounts, the *Shah-Nama*, talked about the birth of an unusual white-skinned child who had been driven away and abandoned in the vicinity of the Caucasus Mountains. We compared that account with the sudden appearance of white-skinned people in the area of the Caucasus range and showed how that child functioned as a symbolic figure, and that the story of his life recounts the early history of white people. In light of the teachings of Elijah Muhammad and as the facts will later show, this account presents an accurate portrayal of the early history of the caucasian race who, due to a "calamity", were stripped of their clothing, removed from association with men and released to live naked and without shelter in the hills of West Asia.

RECORDED IN THE WRITINGS OF DIODORUS

The events outlined of the *Shah-Nama* are also summarized in other sources. Such sources likewise record a series of events identical to those taught by Elijah Muhammad. One example appears in the writings of Diodorus. Diodorus, the ancient writer, admits to having copied his account from even earlier records that had been kept by the ancient Egyptians.

In *Book XL*, Diodorus says that following the appearance ruddy-skinned strangers, Egypt began to suffer from a multitude of troubles and diseases. According to the words of Diodorus, the original people of the land decided that the only way to put an end to their troubles was to round up all of the strangers that they could find and drive them out, across the border. Concerning what happened, Diodorus writes: "When in ancient times a pestilence arose in Egypt, the common people ascribed their trouble to the workings of a divine agency; for indeed with many strangers of all sorts dwelling in their midst....the natives of the land surmised that unless they removed the foreigners, their troubles would never be resolved. At once, therefore, the aliens were" driven from the country..."[67]

Aren't the words of this ancient account identical to what Elijah Muhammad says happened 6,000 years ago following the arrival of the whiteman among the original people?

As to the identity of those strangers, Diodorus refers to them in another place as *a race of lepers* and as people having *white marks on their skin*. In BOOK XXXIV, Diodorus wrote: "For by way of purging the country all persons who had white or leprous marks on their bodies had been assembled and driven across the border, as being under a curse."[68]

What Diodorus here calls "white or leprous marks on their bodies" is shown in his other writings, as well as by the writings of Manetho, the Egyptian priest, to have been in reference to people having white or pale complexions. Many of the writings of the ancient egyptians, hebrews, greeks and others refer to white or pale-complexioned skin as a form of leprosy (a disease characterized by skin ulcers and pigmentary deficit).

The word "pestilence", used in the translation of Diodorus' earlier account, describes the state of affairs brought on by the presence of the strangers. To that extent "pestilence" simply means "a nuisance". Related sources show that in ancient times, acts of mischief or nuisance were also viewed as symptoms of a disease.[69] Since Diodorus uses the word "pestilence" to describe the "troubles" that the original people sought to "resolve", it is clear that a nuisance or state of mischief is intended.[70]

All in all, Diodorus' account, written thousands of years ago, presents a series of historical events identical in every other way to those outlined by the teachings of Elijah Muhammad. They speak of the early presence of a group of white-skinned strangers in the region of the Near East, the troubles that began following their arrival and the way in which the white-skinned strangers were rounded up and driven away from the region.

How well do the events listed in the accounts of Diodorus and the *Shah-Nama* compare with the story of Adam and Eve?

FACTS CONSISTENT WITH THE STORY OF ADAM AND EVE

"So he drove out the man..."
Genesis 3:24

Similar points appear in the Bible's story of Adam and Eve. According to the Bible, Adam was driven out of paradise. But, as to where he went and how he got there, the Bible is silent. Still, it is relevant to ask: What happened to Adam and Eve after they left the Garden of Eden? Were they forced to walk across the desert? Were they destined to live out the rest of their lives in the darkness of a cave? If it can be shown that these things are true then wouldn't this be convincing evidence in support of the teachings of Muhammad?

THE BOOK OF ADAM AND EVE

In Ethiopia, a group of 19th Century explorers uncovered a very ancient document called *The Book of Adam and Eve*. While the exact age of the text remains unknown, many scholars include it as part of *The Lost Books of Eden*. Originally written in Arabic, the text had long ago been translated into Ethiopic. The scholars who first studied it were quick to point out that parts of the text appear in *The Holy Qur'an*, the *Talmud* and elsewhere - showing "the vital role it has played in the original literature of human wisdom."[71]

Of great significance is the fact that *The Book of Adam and Eve* picks up where the Book of Genesis leaves off. In other words, it traces the lives of Adam and Eve from the day they left Eden. And amazingly, it talks about their being forced to walk across the desert; it also describes them living inside the cave that had become their home.

As to the fact that the ancient record speaks of Adam and Eve as having been forced to walk across desert, the text acknowledges: "But when our father Adam, and Eve went out of the garden, they trod the ground on their feet...And when they came to the opening of the gate of the garden, and saw the broad earth spread before them, covered with stones large and small, and with sand, they feared and trembled..."[72]

In as much as a wide space of earth, covered with stones and sand is by definition a desert, and since to "trod the ground on their feet" means they had to walk, then the only reasonable explanation that can be given to these words is that when Adam and Eve were driven out from the Garden, they were forced to walk across a desert. These facts agree with Elijah Muhammad. But, where did Adam's journey across the desert lead him? And, did he end up in living a cave?

The Book of Adam and Eve states that at the end of his trip across the desert, Adam looked down at the uncommon character of his skin and lamented over the trouble that his mischief had gotten him into. Compared with everyone else, Adam's skin looked pale and different. This is also the point at which the text first mentions his destination - a cave. Here are the facts as they have been preserved in *The Book of Adam and Eve*: "And, indeed when Adam looked at his flesh, that was altered, he wept bitterly, he and Eve, over what they had done....And as they came to it Adam wept over himself and said to Eve, "Look at this cave that is to be our prison in this world, and a place of punishment."[73]

So this shows that after they were forced out of the Garden of Eden and made to walk across the desert, Adam and Eve had to live in a cave. According to Elijah Muhammad, the story of Adam and Eve represents the early history of the caucasian race. Could the many similarities which exist between the teachings of Elijah Muhammad and what was recorded thousands of years ago in The Book of Adam and Eve be the result of mere coincidence? Or, is it more likely that there is more depth to the teachings of Muhammad than some have been willing to admit?

Other verses show us what it was like on the inside of Adam's cave: "Adam raised his eyes, and saw the rock and the roof of the cave that covered him overhead, so that he could see neither heaven, nor God's creatures....when in it Adam could not see Eve; he only heard the noise she made. Neither could she see Adam, but heard the noise he made. Then Adam wept, in deep affliction, and smote upon his breast; and he arose and said to Eve, "Where art thou ?" And she said unto him, "Lo,' I am standing in this darkness."[74]

Elijah Muhammad teaches that 6,000 years ago the white race was driven away from the region of the near east into the hills and caves of West Asia. He asserts that the early history of the whiteman is outlined in the story of Adam and Eve. The facts show how closley the story of Adam and Eve conforms to the teachings of Elijah Muhammad. After reviewing the ancient record, and comparing it with the sudden and unexplainable appearance of white people in the area north of the caucasus mountains it is reasonable to conclude that The Book of Adam and Eve agrees with Muhammad.

OUTLINED IN THE HISTORY OF THE JINN

The history of the Jinn is another of the ancient

sources that speak of the early history of the caucasian people. The name "Jinn" means 'hidden' and according to muslim scholars, such as Sayyid Ahmed Khan and others, it is the name given to a group of savage and uncultured people who once lived hidden along the hills of West Asia.[75]

According to the oldest accounts, the Jinn had been allowed to live in Paradise, but then they started trouble and were driven away into the hills and mountains where they were confined to live in caves for a period of 2,000 years. Concerning the early history of the Jinn and the events that led to their expulsion, *The Encyclopaedia of Islam* tells us: "...discord broke out among them and led to bloodshed. God then sent...a legion of angels against the fomenters of trouble, who were thrown back into the mountains."[76]

The book *Approaches to the History of the Qur'an* tells us that the Jinn had been given dominion and were ordered to "inhabit and build up the earth." However, "they became disobedient towards God", so God "dispatched against them a military force of the angels..."[77] Another article in *The Encyclopaedia of Islam* says of them: "But they quarrelled...and finally blood was shed. Allah then sent...a troop of angels against the brawlers who were driven back into the mountains."[78]

Again, the similarities between the history of the

Jinn and the early history of the caucasian people as taught by Elijah Muhammad are strikingly clear. As Muhammad has said of them, the whites were expelled after they had caused trouble and bloodshed in the Holy Land; they were driven away into the hills. The ancient accounts of the jinn, parallel Muhammad's account of the history of white people.

Elijah Muhammad's description of the whiteman being driven away into "the worst and poorest part of our planet earth", is echoed by writer Stephen H. Langdon, who uses nearly identical language when discussing the Jinn. In this regard, Langdon writes: "they rebelled against the gods, and angels drove them to the waste places of the earth."[79]

The ancient sources all acknowledge that the Jinn were driven away from Paradise for causing trouble. More specifically, they had been sent away to live in the hills. What was the name of the area to which the Jinn were sent ?

SENT TO THE CAUCASUS MOUNTAINS

The name of the area into which the Jinn had been driven can be found in a number of sources. In the book, *Iblis in Paradise*, George Roe talks about how Iblis, Leader of the Jinn, and his jinn followers were driven out of Paradise and how they were made to live isolated in an area covered with hills and mountains. One of the significant features of Roe's work is that it reveals the name associated with that mountainous region. Concerning the name of that area, Roe states: "Then Iblis and those who were with him fled from the presence of the Lord. But when Iblis sought to re-enter the garden, he could not find the right path, for whichever way he turned his steps, the topless walls of Mount Kaf towered above him."[80]So according to George Roe the area was called *Kaf.*

B. Allen Donaldson, author of *The Wild Rue*, also acknowledges "Kaf" to be the name of the mountains into which the Jinn were driven. On page 35 Donaldson says of the Jinn, that they lived "isolated behind the mountains of Kaf..."[81]

Where are the mountains of Kaf? "Kaf" is the ancient name used to identify the Caucasus Mountains. The book, *Twelve Secrets of the Caucasus* bears this out. There, Essad-Bey, a man who grew up in the Caucasus Mountains wrote all about the history of that region and said of the Caucasus Mountains: "The ancients called these mountains Kaf..."[82]

So the Jinn were driven into the area of the Caucasus Mountains. Again this is consistent with the teachings of Muhammad. According to the words of Muhammad, the Caucasians were driven to the border of West Asia and released near the area of what is today called Turkey. Turkey is that country which lies on the border of the Caucasus Mountains. Likewise, the Caucasus Mountains are the same ones named in the *Shah-Nama* as being the place to where the white-skinned child had been sent. The Caucasus Mountains are located to the north of the Near East, in the area called West Asia.

THE CAUCASIAN PEOPLE

There is no doubt but that the history of the Jinn is an outline of the early history of the Caucasian race. Their entire description fits the whiteman perfectly. For instance, in the Maulawi Sher Ali translation of *The Holy Qur'an*, the Jinn are identified as a group of white-skinned people who long ago lived in the hills and caves of europe. In the glossary section of the english translation, under the word "Jinn", the definition reads: "The inhabitants of northern hilly tracts of Europe, of white and red color, whom other peoples looked upon as beings separate from other human beings and who lived detached from the civilized peoples of Asia but who were destined to make great material progress in the latter days and to lead a great revolt against religion....Wild and savage peoples who...lived in caves and hollows of the earth and were subject to no rules of conduct."[83]

This leaves little room for doubt as to the true identity of the Jinn - they are the Caucasians. Other sources verify these facts and portray the Jinn as a pale-skinned, blonde race of people. Many of the white tribes who today, still inhabit the area of the Caucasus Mountains, such as the Kurds, are often spoken of as their descendants. In the book, *Children of the Jinn*, M. Khan chronicles the history of the Kurdish people and talks about how their history is connected to the history of the Jinn being driven away into the mountains. Khan characterizes the history of the Jinn as one "which tries to explain how such a fair-skinned, light-haired people...came to be living in the mountains that lie astride the borders separating present-day Iran, Iraq, Turkey, and the USSR."[84]

In addition to the Kurds, other groups who live in the region of the Caucasus not only acknowledge the fact that their ancestors arrived there after leaving the Near East but, more than that, they admit that their ancestors departed from that region during the time of a calamity - when the original people were fighting and killing one another. The Armenians are among those who openly acknowledge that fact. In respect to how the Armenians ended up living in the area of the

Caucasus Mountains, the highly esteemed Moses of Khoren, the ancient scholar and father of Armenian history wrote: "...the brave Haig, the founder of the Armenian nation, rebelled...during the civil wars among the Sumerian states, moved northward with his son Armenach and his followers, and settled in the Ararat region."[85]

This shows that the ancestors of the Armenians left the Near East during a time when the people were fighting and killing one another. Concerning the historical relevance of the above account, S. Hoogasian-Villa confirms that these facts are still accepted by the Armenians of today.

In summation, the ancient record tells us that after the Jinn had caused trouble and bloodshed, they were driven away from Paradise and forced to live in the hills of West Asia. Both the Kurds and the Armenians admit to being descendants of the Jinn; both groups are white; both live in the hills of West Asia and both insist that their ancestors traveled to that area from the region of the Near East during the time of a calamity when the original people of the Near East were fighting and killing one another. Is there any doubt but that the history of the Jinn corroborates the teachings of Elijah Muhammad?

RE-ENACTED IN THE ATONEMENT

In his book, *Message to the Blackman*, Elijah Muhammad includes the name "Azazel" to be one of many used to describe the white race.[86] According to hebrew tradition, Azazel is one of the names given to the leader of the devils - it is the hebrew name for *Iblis*, leader of the Jinn.

Once a year, on the eve of the Jewish Day of Atonement, a ceremony is traditionally performed in which a goat (Azazel) is tied to a rope and led away from the people, out into the desert and abandoned in a place of hills and rocks. The ceremony of the atonement, handed down from generation to generation, is a re-enactment of the early history of the caucasian people.

Instructions describing the commencement of the ceremony can be found in the 16th chapter of *Leviticus*. There, verses 21 and 22 state: "He shall put both hands on the goat's head and confess over it all the evils, sins and rebellions of the people of Israel, and so transfer them to the goat's head. Then the goat is to be driven off into the desert by a man appointed to do it. The goat will carry all their sins away with him into some uninhabited land."[87]

Concerning the history of Azazel, *The Encyclopaedia Judaica* asserts that long ago he and his followers had been driven away into "a land which was cut off", "an area of rocks and cliffs" and "a place of hard mountains."[88]When all of these facts are brought together, it becomes clear that the history of Azazel is identical to the history of Iblis and the Jinn. Like Iblis, Azazel was bound, driven across the desert and released in a land of rocks, cliffs, hills and mountains.

Volume 3 of *The Encyclopaedia Judaica* compares the ceremony of the atonement to another Old Testament ceremony wherein white birds are used in connection with the purification of lepers. Regarding that connection the encyclopaedia states: "...the two goats can be compared to the birds used in the purification ritual of the leper..."(Lev. 14:4-7).[89]That the goats, white birds and lepers are all intended as representing white people is also clear.

In his book, *The Golden Bough*, James Frazer shows how the animals used in these various ceremonies function as stand-ins for the people who perform the ceremony. On page 210, Frazer notes: "Modern Jews sacrifice a white cock on the eve of the Day of Atonement, nine days after the beginning of their New Year. The father of the family knocks the cock thrice against his own head, saying, "Let this cock be a *substitute for me, let it take my place*, let death be laid upon this cock, but a happy life bestowed on me and on all Israel."

Then he cuts its throat and dashes the bird violently on the ground."[90]

IN THE CAVES FOR 2,000 YEARS

A more thorough understanding of the history of Azazel can be had by examining *The Book of Enoch*. For 500 years *The Book of Enoch* was accepted as part of the Bible. It was accepted as such by Jesus, Peter, Paul and by all of Jesus's other followers. But later, the Church took *The Book of Enoch* out of the Bible. An article discussing the history of *The Book of Enoch* appeared in the Dec. 7, 1935 edition of *Liberty Magazine*. Showing how other parts of the Bible had been changed or altogether removed from the Scriptures by cunning European leaders, the article reads in part: "For more than a century, scholars and church officials debated as to whether or not certain gospels, epistles and apocalypses should be included. For instance, it was long debated which to include in the canon, the Book of Revelation, or the Book of Enoch, which had been accepted as Scripture by Jesus and Paul, and the whole Christian Church, for several centuries. Revelation finally won out, and became the last book of the Bible. The Book of Enoch, under a stigma because deemed uncanonical, gradually dropped out of use, and finally disappeared."[91]

Fortunately, additional copies of *The Book of Enoch* were safeguarded by the Ethiopians until 1772, when they were "re-discovered". One of the significant things that a study of *The Book of Enoch* does is it confirms that after Azazel and his followers were driven away across the desert, they were made to live in the caves for 2,000 years.

According to the ancient text, a group of Angels were instructed to tie up Azazel and to propel him and his followers out into the desert. Then, the book says, they were taken up into the hills where they were confined to live in the caves (beneath rough and jagged rocks), for a period of 2,000 years. *The Book of Enoch* narrates the events this way: "Bind Azazel by his hands and his feet, and throw him into the darkness: and make an opening in the desert, which is in Dudael, and cast him therein. And place upon him rough and jagged rocks and cover him with darkness and let him stay there....*bind them for seventy generations* in the hills of the earth..."[92]

As *The American College Dictionary* points out, a "generation" is a period of time equal to 30 years. Seventy generations equal just over 2,000 years.[93] Thus, *The Book of Enoch*, (the same one that Jesus accepted as part of the bible), verifies the precise amount of time that Azazel and his followers (white people) were forced to live in the caves. The period of time stated in *The Book of Enoch* matches up perfectly with what has been stated by Muhammad. Is this just another coincidence?

ACKNOWLEDGED BY TIBETAN BUDDHISTS

At the beginning of each New Year, the Buddhists of Tibet perform an identical ceremony in which these same events are re-enacted. However, the Buddhists do not use a goat or any other animal as a substitute, they use real people. The ancient Tibetan ceremony is rich in symbolism: it retains the use of an apron or coat of skin; it employs the use of the 2 colors - black and white; it utilizes the symbolism of the number six; it illustrates how the person to be driven away had disrespected the ruler and caused a disruption in the market place and that as a result he was chased away by the people and made to live as a savage in a land of hills and mountains.

The Buddhists say that long ago a wicked ruler showed up among the people and began to disrupt the citizens of the city by his use of mischief. Called the *King of Years*, they say he tried to challenge the authority of the original king and that he sat in the market place and helped himself to anything he wanted. This is all outlined in the

Buddhist ceremony. A description of it can be found in James G. Frazer's *The Golden Bough*. There, Frazer writes:

"The man is not killed purposely, but the ceremony he undergoes often proves fatal....his face is painted half white, half black. Thus grotesquely disguised, and carrying a coat of skin on his arm, he is called the King of Years, and sits daily in the market place, where he helps himself to whatever he likes and goes about shaking a black yak's tail over the people....He then ridicules the Jaino (the ruler), saying to him, "What we perceive through the five senses is no illusion. All you teach is untrue." ....The ruler then shows the King of Years a set of dice which are marked with all sixes.... When he sees the finger of Providence thus plainly pointed against him, the King of Years is terrified and flees away upon a white horse, with a white dog, a white bird, salt, and so forth, which have all been provided for him by the government....The whole populace pursues him....Thus driven out of the city, he is...surrounded by monstrous and terrific images of devils...and wild beasts. Thence he goes away into the mountains... where he has to remain an outcast..."[94]

Would all the above mentioned cultures record the same historical events and re-enact the same ceremonies if it were all meaningless? The evidence goes to support the teachings of Elijah Muhammad.

CHAPTER 6

THE HILLS AND CAVES OF WEST ASIA

This chapter examines the evidence surrounding what happened after the caucasians arrived in the hills of West Asia; it talks about how they were "roped in" and takes a look at some of the probable methods used to keep them beyond the borders of civilization.

Concerning what took place after the whites arrived in West Asia, Muhammad writes: "Once there, they were roped in, to keep them out of Paradise. To make sure, the Muslims, who lived along the borders of East and West Asia, were ordered to patrol the border to keep Yakub's devils in West Asia, so that the original nation of black men could live in peace; and that the devils could be alone to themselves, to do as they pleased, as long as they didn't try crossing the East border."[95]

What means were used to keep the caucasians from crossing back over into civilization? How were the guards able to keep the Caucasians back beyond the border?

THE WALLS OF THE CAUCASUS

Travel in and out of the Caucasus mountains is

possible only through a small number of narrow passages. The facts show that after the whites had arrived in the area of the caucasus Mountains, an extensive series of walls and fortresses were erected, sealing off all exits, coming down, out of the hills. The evidence shows that massive structures of stone and wood covered with iron were placed along the narrow passages thereby blocking any travel into or out of that part of the world. The facts also show that these walls had been put into place for the purpose of keeping the white tribes from crossing back over into civilization. High atop the towering walls, flanked by steep cliffs and insurmountable barriers of rock and ice, armed guards stood watch while others patrolled surrounding regions of the border.

Known as the "Gates of the Caucasus" or the "Caucasian Walls ," descriptions of them appear in the works of many writers, including the roman encyclopedist, Pliny. Once, deep in the heart of the Caucasus mountains, Pliny came face to face with some of the remains of these ancient fortresses. In a report on the incident, Pliny described a gigantic iron gate, which stood, he said, blocking one of the passages, "in the middle of the Caucasus range." Writing in his book, *Natural History*, Pliny commented on the historical significance of these ancient gates and walls, stating that they had long ago been "erected for the purpose of barring the passage of the innumerable tribes."[96]

H.N. Wethered, the historian, also talks about how a series of fortresses had once been used as barricades in all the exits along the Caucasus Mountains. On page 270 of his book, *The Mind of the Ancient World*, Wethered affirms: "The gates of the Caucasus were barred with beams shod with iron...Here was Cumania, a fortress erected to keep back the savage tribes beyond."[97] Concerning the gate at the passage of Cumania, Wethered noted that it's original purpose was to rope-off Europe from the rest of the world. In this regard, Wethered wrote: "...so Europe and Asia were divided by many straits and narrow passages....(here) we see the habitable ;world severed, as it were, into two parts by the partition guarded by the two gates."[98]

The walls and gates mentioned in the writings of Pliny and Wethered are only a few of the many whose remains can still be found, spread-out over the entire stretch of the Caucasus range - a distance of 666 miles. That all of the narrow passages were roped-off and guarded by the same method, is further attested to in other writings. In the year 1781, an explorer journeyed into the Caucasus mountains for the purpose of inspecting the Walls of the Caucasus for himself. What he found is recorded on pages 33 and 34 of the book *Tagebuch*:

"...there in front of us was a wall and tower, partly fallen, built right across the defile, here only 20 fathoms broad with an impassable mountain on either side. Remains such as these of frontier fortresses I have found right through the Caucasus from one sea to the other in all the narrowest defiles giving passage through the mountains."[99]

This is saying that the Walls of the Caucasus were *a series of walls* and that those walls blocked *all* of the exits along that area *from one sea to the other*. This is important because it goes to show that the Caucasian tribes were literally "roped in" and that they were in fact prevented from crossing back over into civilization.

Other sources show that the area around the Caucasian Walls were kept under constant watch by armed guards who in ancient times stood and defended the border from attack. According to the history of the Caucasus Mountains, the guards developed a system of communication whereby they were able to pass messages back and forth among one another, from one end of the border all the way over to the other. A statement verifying this can be found in the book, *The Rugged Flanks of Caucasus*. There, writer John F. Baddely said about the men who once guarded the border along the Caucasus Mountains: "...at one time the sentinels stationed along it at regular intervals could pass a message vocally all the way from Derbend to Constantinople in an incredibly short space of time."[100]

What of the ancient builders, who developed this means of defending the border?

One writer, a professor from Oxford University, talks about the high degree of planning that had to have gone into the construction of the Caucasian Walls. Praising the organizational skill of its builders, the professor pointed out: "...the fortification of these narrow defiles was the simplest, most natural and least expensive in regard to upkeep of any possible method of frontier defense in the Caucasus."[101]

Yet, despite such a well-organized defense, roving gangs of caucasians would from time to time manage to slip pass weak spots along the border. Hanging on to the backs of horses, the lucky savages would be free to pillage their way southward. William Hardy McNeil wrote about the persistence with which the whiteman tried to breakthrough the guarded region and of their constant attempts to reach and plunder the civilizations of the south. In his book, *A World History*, McNeil writes: "Raiding the richer, civilized regions lying to the south of the steppe zone was a constant temptation. Any weakening in the guard which civilized rulers maintained against such raids was quickly discovered by casual parties of nomad horsemen, probing southward on the lookout for whatever they could pick up."[102]

THE DESERT BANDITS

What was the result of those who were able to sneak pass the border? Over the course of many years the roads running along the desert became infested with pockets of Caucasian bandits. Hiding-out along roads and caravan routes, the robbers survived by preying upon travelers, often murdering and stripping their victims of their possessions. The records of the region are replete with references describing how the the marauders would often hide inside a hole or behind some bush near an isolated stretch of road and then jump out to beat the weary traveler with sticks while robbing him of his cargo. One report, from the records of ancient egypt, says of them:

"...the ways are not guarded roads. Men sit in the bushes until the benighted traveler comes, to take away his burden and steal what is on him. He is presented with the blows of a stick and slain wrongfully."[103]

Other sources from Mesopotamia tell of similar

violence inflicted upon the original people by gangs of whites who had come down from out of the caves. One source in particular states:

"In a cave in the depths of the underworld they have grown up....They are not acquainted with compassion and mercy....They cause disasters on the roads, on the roads of the land they lie and crouch."[104]

On page 35 of the book *Myths and Legends of Babylonia and Assyria*, Lewis Spence quotes a source from ancient Sumeria describing how "the devils of the desert" would frequently lay obstacles across the road and wait until an unsuspecting person stopped to remove the obstacles, at which time the nomads would sneak up from behind and strike him down. This is what the ancient writer intended when he wrote:

"The evil udug, which makes the solitary ways difficult to pass over, which goes forth in secret, covers up the ways,...the robber, who cannot be forced back...they have struck down the wayfaring man as in a storm."[105]

The infestation of the deserts and the resulting danger along the roads and caravan routes occurred during the period of reconstruction which was outlined in chapter 1. It was also during that same time that other walls, besides those that guarded the border, had to be constructed. The additional walls were stretched-out along the deserts. Their purpose was to keep the bandits from closing in on the reconstructed towns and cities. In Volume 2 of his book *Historical Researches into the Politics, Intercourse and Trade of the Carthaginians, Ethiopians and Egyptians*, Arnold Heeren discusses one such wall that had been constructed along the desert in Mesopotamia. He says that through the presence of such wall the nomads were held back from entering civilization, having been "cut off by a wall of bricks, cemented with bitumen, which ran obliquely across the plain from the Euphrates to the Tigris, and was commonly called the Median Wall."[106]

That this was just one of many such barricades that had to be errected along the desert to keep the whites away, is attested to in the words of Heeren who said of the Median Wall: "Like *many other structures* of the same kind in Asia, it appears to have been designed to repress the incursions of the barbarous hordes, which infested the desert without....The mountains which bounded Mesopotamia to the north were in a great measure occupied by rude and warlike tribes..."[107]

The ancient writer Manetho explains that a similar wall had to be erected along the desert bordering Egypt and that it was guarded and kept under constant patrol by "as many as 240,000 heavy-armed men."[108]

So the evidence shows that after the Caucasians had arrived in the hills of West Asia they were roped in by armed guards who patrolled the border near the area of the Caucasus Mountains. The exits along those mountains had been sealed off by very large gates and walls. Over the course of many years additional precautions became necessary, particularly in the deserts which had become infested with pockets of nomadic bandits. These are a few of the many facts related to the teachings of Elijah Muhammad

ORAL TRADITIONS OF THE CAUCASUS MOUNTAINS

In *Twelve Secrets of the Caucasus*, Essad-Bey talks about the people who used to inhabit that area. On page 128, he says of them: "What persuaded them to hunt out such an inhospitable region, it is hard to conceive. The very places which were least suitable for human occupation...Any gorge to which light of day never penetrated, or any rock hard upon the edge of a precipice, surrounded on three sides by the eternal snow, was their preferred abode."[109] This description shows that the Caucasus Mountains is not the kind of place where people would desire to live.

The recollection of ancient life along the hills and caves of West Asia is preserved in the oral traditions of the region. Throughout those traditions, the whiteman's "imprisonment" in the caves is repeatedly alluded to. In their most common form, the ancient accounts tell of an evil ruler who, having fought against *the gods*, was roped with an iron chain and compelled to spend the rest of his days locked away inside of a cave. Again these accounts chronicle the early history of the whites and tell of the circumstances that caused them to have to live there.

In one sense, the Caucasian oral traditions can be looked at as a continuation of the earlier accounts dealing with the birth of the white-skinned child. We recall that his arrival led to a calamity and as a result he was driven away and left in the hills of West Asia.

One of the oral traditions from the Caucasus Mountains talks about a cruel king who kept robbing and murdering until he was driven away from the people and locked inside of a cave. It is also said that he shared his cave with a dog. Of that tradition, Essad-Bey says: "But the King kept constantly attacking... pillaging, murdering, and robbing. So the Lord of the World took pity and seized the cruel king and incarcerated him in the depths of the rocks of Ararat. He was bound with an iron chain. His favorite dog alone shared his prison."[110]

In another variant of the tradition, the evil ruler is said to have been so thoroughly isolated that his only knowledge of the outside world came from the guard who watched over him. Summarizing this account, Essad-Bey writes:

"Protected by a guard, shut up within the mountains, sits an old king. Once every hundred years, the king asks: "Does grass still grow upon the earth, and do the lambs still find increase?" When the guard has told him that this is so, the King moans and strikes with his fist upon the walls of his cavern."[111]

As John F. Baddely points out, in none of the oral traditions does the release of the captive bring happiness to Man, but in each case, Baddely reminds us, "evil is directly foretold, or at least implied."[112]That the migration of the whiteman out of the hills of West Asia should be looked upon as an unhappy event is perfectly understandable when viewed from the perspective of the many cultures with whom the whites would later come into contact.

M.H. Ananikian, the Turkish historian, shares one of the oral traditions that tell of the evil which was to result from the release of the captive. In an article appearing in *The Mythology of All Races*, the evil ruler is here called a "changeling son". Pointing out the effects of his release, the article tells us: "The people told about him that he was chained in a cave of Massis (Ararat) with iron fetters which were constantly gnawed at by two dogs. When they are broken he will come out to rule over the world or to destroy it."[113]

Showing how widespread these traditions are, Baddely shows how the same history is reflected in the greek tale of Prometheus whom legend records as having been fastened with iron chains to the savage rocks of the Caucasus. Of Prometheus, Baddely recalls: "His faithful companion, a giant hound, licks unceasingly the iron chains by which his master is fastened to the rock."[114]

As we have seen, many of the oral traditions note that dogs were among the inhabitants of the caves. Writing on page 119 of *Message to the Blackman*, Muhammad explains: "They tamed some of these dogs to live in the caves with their families, to help protect them from the wild beasts. After a time, the dog held a high place among the family because of his fearlessness to attack the enemies of his master."[115]

LIFE INSIDE THE CAVES

Left without shelter, the Caucasians began to live in the innumerable caves which nature had carved in the limestone hills. Thousands of the small caverns can still be found along the slopes of the Caucasus Mountains. Covering an area of several hundred miles, their openings face the north. Today, they are called "the caverns of the northern caucasus".[116]

In his book, *Cave Hunting: Researches on the Evidence of Caves, Respecting the Early Inhabitants of Europe*, W. Boyd Dawkins offers his perspective on the subject. Concerning the isolation and the circumstances which led them to seek protection in the caves, Dawkins writes: "...compelled by the pressure of some great calamity, to flee for refuge, and to lead a half-savage life in these inclement caves....they were cut off from the civilization to which they had been accustomed."[117]

A clear picture of the caves and their inhabitants is presented in *The Holy Qur'an*. In the chapter called *Al-Kahf*, the Qur'an states:

"And thou mightest see the sun, when it rose, decline from their Cave to the right, and when it set leave them behind on the left, while they were in a wide space thereof....And thou mightest think them awake while they were asleep, and we turned them about to the right and to the left, with their dog outstretching its paws at the entrance. If thou didst look at them, thou wouldst be filled with awe because of them."[118]

In addition to the small caverns which nature had carved in the limestone slopes, the early europeans also lived in man-made holes or hollows. The hollow was a simple tunnel, 10 to 15 feet deep and wide enough for a man to crawl through. At the end of the tunnel was an underground nest or den. Like the natural cave, the hollow offered the whiteman a place of refuge and safety, where he could hide, eat and sleep.[119]

In times of bitter cold, the inhabitants of the hollow could cover the entrance with excrement or manure. This was a popular way of keeping warm during the winter months. In addition to blocking out the cold air, the steam produced beneath the rotting excrement served to warm and humidify the inside of the hollow.

Ancient sources indicate that keeping warm by staying beneath massive piles of stench was common throughout many parts of Europe and that the custom was still practiced as late as the time of Tacitus. Tacitus, the ancient historian, traveled extensively throughout the interior of europe and wrote about some of the wild tribes who still inhabited that region in his day. In his book, *Germania*, Tacitus said of them: "They also have the habit of hollowing out underground caves, which they cover with masses of manure....Such shelters temper the keenness of the frosts."[120]

In *Book IV*, Xenophon Anbasis mentions the underground tunnels having been used in the Caucasus Mountains. Xenophon Anabasis goes on to say that the white inhabitants once shared those tunnels with "goats, sheep, cattle, fowls, and their young" and that in those tunnels "all the animals were reared and took their fodder."[121] The suggestion is that in order to protect the animals from theft, it was necessary to keep them underground.

In *Prehistoric Antiquities of the Aryan Peoples*, Dr. O. Schrader also discusses the ancient use of "subterranean dwellings, *i.e.*, dwellings dug in the earth, the existence of which is recorded amongst numerous Indo-Germanic peoples, and which afforded protection alike against the summer's heat and the winter's cold."[122]

So it is a fact that after they arrived in the hills of West Asia the whites were compelled to seek refuge in the caves.

Concerning the way of life that had developed as a result of their isolation, Elijah Muhammad writes:

"They were punished by being deprived of divine guidance, for 2,000 years which brought them almost into the family of wild beasts - going upon all fours; eating raw and unseasoned food; living in caves and treetops, climbing and jumping from one tree to another."[123]

Is this an exaggeration or is it an accurate characterization of an historical event?

THE LAND OF MAZANDARAN

The most accessible part of the Caucasus Mountains is that section known in ancient times as *Mazandaran.* Located between the Alburz Mountains and the Caspian Sea, Mazandaran was during that day, cold, wet and heavily wooded. It is from Mazandaran that many of the first eye-witness accounts have been recieved. Those accounts describe life beyond the Caucasian Walls. An excellent source of these first-hand accounts appear in a collection of writings called the Pahlavi texts.

The *Jamasp-Namak*, one of the ancient Pahlavi texts, relates that in Mazandaran the whiteman had fallen so low in his living habits that he had started to resemble the wild animals.[124] *According to the Jamasp-Namak,* behind the Caucasus Mountains in the land of Mazandaran lived a race of cave-dwellers whose members were considered by others to be non-human.

The Pahlavi document called the *Dinkard describes them as filthy and living in holes*. There they are also reputed to have practiced habits so shameful that they were believed to be other than human beings until it was discovered that they spoke a form of language. Concerning the ancient discussions that once took place as to whether the people of Mazandaran were human and how it was finally decided that they were, the *Dinkard* states:

"And they also said this about the vileness of the Mazandarans, and the wretched state of the people of this region...Since their habits are thus, since they are filthy - that is dirt is theirs - possessing holes - that is holes are theirs - and having appellations - that is they call to one another - we men think, and consider upon this, that they are human beings."[125]

Other ancient sources refer to the same people as devils or "dev". In a commentary on the Dev (devils) as they appear in the ancient *Zend Avesta*, M.N. Dhalla explains that the *Devils of Mazandaran* were simply the barbarians who later "poured down in great numbers and pillaged the possessions of the Iranians."[126]

In this same regard the *Shah-Nama* recalls a time

when the hills of Mazandaran were inhabited by a race of what it calls "white devils". As to the real identity of the white devils of Mazandaran, A.G. Warner explains that the *Shah-Nama* uses the term "White Demon" as "a personification of the Mazandaranis rendered pale by the unhealthiness of their climate."[127]

B. Allen Donaldson also speaks of the Dev, saying that they were a race of wild men who once ran around wearing the horns of animals. In *The Wild Rue*, Donaldson says of them: "...the div were merely wild men of the jungle of Mazandaran, who fought with wild animals. And when they killed these animals they took the skins for clothing and wore them, head, horns, tails and all."[128]

Donaldson's characterization of these early Caucasians as "wild men" who wore horns does much to explain the many accounts of "the horned men" that are found throughout the records of the ancient world. Such accounts come to us mostly from the region of the Zagros mountains, but sightings have been reported from as far away as India. The accounts all tell of a race of hairy, cannibalistic horned men who lived in holes in the ground and ate their food raw. An example fitting this description is preserved in an oral account recorded by Verrier Elwin in his book, *Tribal Myths of Orissa*. That account reads:

"Far away to the west is a great mountain, too steep to climb. Here live the horned men. They are naked and their bodies are covered with long hair...If they meet a man who has no horns, they kill and eat him immediately. Their wives are very fat...They live in tiny houses, built below ground level. They do not know how to cook but eat their food raw."[129]

That all of these eye-witness accounts describe the whites of Mazandaran in such vivid terms only establishes that Elijah Muhammad's description cannot be called an exageration. These accounts help to illustrate the depths to which the whites had fallen following their expulsion from civilization.

Lastly, the *Shah-Nama* talks about a black warrior named Rustem who is said to have gone up into the hills of Mazandaran and to have waged war against the people of that area. According to the *Shah-Nama,* Rustem was informed that in order for him to reach "the caves of the White Demon and his warrior chiefs", he would have to travel beyond the guards who patrolled along the narrow passages leading up into the mountains. As to the directions given to Rustem, the *Shah-Nama* says:

"The road is straight before thee - reach the Seven Mountains and there thou wilt discern the various groups which guard the awful passage. Farther on, within a deep and horrible recess frowns the White Demon."[130]

Rustem's journey into that dangerous part of the world also gives us a picture of life in the hills of Mazandaran, for we are told that Rustem "Hurried on until he came to the Haft-koh, or Seven Mountains. There he found numerous companies of Demons; and coming to one of the caverns, saw it crowded with the same awful beings."[131]

Again, how closely do the ancient accounts compare with Elijah Muhammad's description of the whites when they lived in the hills of West Asia?

Objections are often raised regarding Elijah Muhammad's use of the term "devils" in connection white people. Some claim Muhammad's use of that term is based on prejudice, others say it is based on real facts. What is the early history of the term "devil"? And when was it first used as a name for white people?

WHITES REFERRED TO AS DEVILS IN ANCIENT EGYPT

The issue is: Whether the *devil* was originally used as a name for white people. In chapter 6 we saw how the *Shah-Nama*, the *Zend Avesta* and other sources referred to the whites who had been compelled to live in the hills of West Asia as either "devils", "Dev" or "Demons". Countless other examples could be given, such as the writings of Zarathustra, who wrote extensively about what he perceived as the need to fight against the Caucasian invaders who he too referred to as devils.

But some of the earliest evidence available to the student of history appears in the records of ancient Egypt. The ancient Egyptians referred to the devil or Satan under various names. The three most common of those names were: Seth, Typhon and Apopis. It is also a fact that throughout the writings of ancient Egypt the Caucasian people are referred to as the "Typhonians" or the "People of Seth." When Diodorus spoke of a group of "foreigners" who had been driven out of Egypt, he described them as "men the color of Typhon". Similar language can be found in the writings of Manetho, the egyptian priest, who on many occasions referred to the whites as "Typhonians". In english, such names mean "the devils". So the earliest evidence suggests that the ancient Egyptians viewed the caucasian people as a race of devils.[132]

What are some of the examples in which the "Typhonians" are mentioned? Do such writings also show the Typhonians (devils) to have been white people? In his book *The Sky-Religion in Egypt*, G.A. Wainwright, talks about the discovery of fragments from an ancient egyptian text in which the Typhonians or Followers of Seth are alluded to.

On page 33 of his book, Wainwright comments in this regard:

"A remarkable and hitherto unparalleled text has just been published by Gardiner, and though terribly fragmentary a good deal may be gleaned from it. Among other things it shows that as late as the Nineteenth Dynasty a section of the Egyptians were known to be 'Followers of Seth', Typhonians, by certain marks and characteristics. Of such it is said: 'The god in him is Seth'....Another badly damaged sentence mentions a 'red man' and his hair."[133]

What did the writer mean by the words "a red man and his hair" ? What were the characteristics by which the Typhonians were known?

The "marks and characteristics" that set apart the Typhonians or devils from the original people of egypt were their hair and the pinkish or red color of their complexion. This much at least is admitted to by Wainwright who talks about one Typhonian in particular, whom he calls Nitocris, when he comments on her pale complexion. That the "red men" or Typhonians in Egypt were white people, Wainwright notes: "...in having a fair complexion Nitocris was clearly one of the red Typhonians who were sacrificed by fire for the good of the people."[134]

The above quote shows two things: first, that the people known as the Typhonians had pale or ruddy complexions; and secondly, that those pale-skinned people were, from time to time, rounded up and killed "for the good of the people." What other evidence is there to support this claim ?

Throughout the history of ancient Egypt, many campaigns were waged against the caucasians who, as history shows, repeatedly attacked egypt and subjected the original people to the most reprehensible atrocities. Often the people of Egypt found it necessary to fight back against the aggressors. Thus, many of the ancient texts speak of times when the original people would gather up all of the white people (Typhonians) that they could find and either cut off their heads or burn them alive. So it was with good reason that in Section 73 of *De Iside et Osiride*, Plutarch acknowledged the following: "For truly, as Manetho has recorded, they used to burn living men to ashes in Eileithyiapolis, calling them Typhonians, and they used to scatter and dispose of their ashes by winnowing."[135]

Regarding this same matter, Diodorus wrote: "anciently men who were similarly colored to Typhon were sacrificed by the kings."[136]

The rounding up and killing of the Caucasians by the kings of ancient Egypt is exactly what Wainwright was describing when he wrote: "Though in the New Kingdom at the Festivals of

Hoeing the Earth the Seth-sacrifices clearly had their heads cut off, it is equally clear that on other occasions the sacrifice had been by fire."[137]

In as much as the evidence from Egypt clearly shows that the term "devil" was once just another name for white people, and since that fact tends to substantiate what Elijah Muhammad has stated, then anyone objecting to Muhammad's use of that term, on strictly historical grounds, should be able to offer some kind of historical evidence capable of out-weighing the above facts. If that evidence cannot be produced then thier objection must be viewed as unreasonable.

MUSA

How were the Caucasians able to leave the hills and caves of West Asia and to begin their climb toward civilization? Elijah Muhammad teaches that a man named Musa was sent to lead the white race back into the light of civilization. So in 2000 B.C., Musa travelled into the interior of europe. There he began the tremendous task of introducing the caucasian people to the laws of civilization. Concerning Musa's work among the savage tribes, Elijah Muhammad writes:

"After 2000 years of living as a savage, Allah raised up Musa (Moses) to bring the white race again into civilization: to take their place as rulers....He brought them out of the caves...taught them to wear clothes; how to cook their food; how to season it with salt; what beef they should kill and eat..."[138]

On page 93 of Message to the Blackman, Muhammad says that Musa lived in about 2000 B.C. It was also in regard to this same period of time that Chester Starr wrote: "...for unknown reasons, the group went into a ferment shortly before 2000 BC. and started spilling out all over Europe and western Asia."[139]

In about 2000 B.C. the whites first began to migrate out of the hills of West Asia. Historians have been unable explain the reasons behind their movements. Could the work of Musa, as taught by Elijah Muhammad, help to explain their sudden awakening?

In *Message to the Blackman*, Elijah Muhammad informs us that Musa or Moses, went over to the whites from out of Egypt and that when he first found them they were still living in the caves.[140] Other details from the life of Musa and his perilous journey into the european wilderness are outlined in the book *The Story of Mankind*, by Hendrik Willem van Loon. On page 17, van Loon talks about the man from Egypt who first led the whites out of the caves and into the light of civilization. On page 17 van Loon writes:

"These earliest ancestors of ours who lived in the great European wilderness were rapidly learning many new things. It is safe to say that in the course of time they would have given up the ways of savages and would have developed a civilization of their own. But suddenly there came an end to their isolation. They were discovered.

"A traveler from an unknown southland who had dared to cross the sea and the high mountain passes had found his way to the wild people of the European continent. He came from Africa. His home was in Egypt."[141]

So van Loon credits Musa with having travelled from Egypt up into the European wilderness and with leading the whiteman out of his savage condition.

The ancient writer Diodorus agrees that Musa was an Egyptian. In one place Diodorus even calls him an Egyptian Priest. According to the ancient writer, Musa had set out on a journey to the north where he established a colony among a people whom Diodorus calls *a race of Lepers*. There, he tells us, Musa taught them how to follow directions and prepared them to make ready for war.[142]

Still more facts relating to the life of Musa can be found in the writings of the ancient Egyptians. Such writings tell of a man known as Ozar Sef who had left his home, where he lived in the city of Heliopolis. They say that he changed his name to Musa or Moses and went off to teach the Caucasians. The same records point out that after he had given them a code of laws they came down out of the hills and launched an attack against Egypt. For that reason, Manetho's account of the whiteman's invasion of Egypt is particularly significant. After discussing the brutality that the white invaders showed toward the original people of Egypt, Manetho turns his attention to the way in which they had first been led into the knowledge of civilization. Concerning their attack on Egypt and the Egyptian who had taught them, Manetho writes:

"Not only did they set cities and villages on fire, not only did they pillage the temples and mutilate the images...but not content with that, they habitually used the very sanctuaries as kitchens for roasting the venerated sacred animals, and forced the priests and prophets to slaughter them and cut their throats, and then turned them out naked. It is said that the priest who gave them a constitution and a code of laws was a native of Heliopolis, named Osarsiph after the Heliopolitan god Osiris, and that when he went over to this people he changed his name and was called Moses."[143]

That Manetho records the whites as having invaded Egypt after they had been taught by Musa is perfectly consistent with the words of Muhammad who on page 104 of *Message to the Blackman* writes: "They rose up from the caves and hillsides of Europe, went back to Asia, and have ruled nine-tenths of that great continent."[144]

CONCLUSION

Throughout this book we have presented evidence which speaks to the accuracy of the teachings of Elijah Muhammad. We have tried to show that the teachings of Muhammad, concerning the origins and early history of the white race are consistent with the facts and with the writings of ancient traditional accounts. It is my hope that this book will help to inspire others to become more interested in learning more about the teachings of Elijah Muhammad.

REFERENCES

1. Riane Eisler, *The Chalice and the Blade* (San Francisco: Harper & Row, 1987), pp. 43-44.
2. James Mellaart, *The Neolithic of the Middle East* (New York: Scribner, 1975), p.280.
3. Chester G. Starr, *A History of the Ancient World* (New York: Oxford Univ. Press, 1983), p. 81.
4. Marija Gimbutas, "*Old Europe c. 7000-3500 B.C.: The Earliest European Civilization Before the Infiltration of the Indo-European Peoples*" in *Journal of Indo-European Studies*, vol. 1, Spring 1973.
5. Riane Eisler, *The Chalice and the Blade* (San Francisco: Harper & Row, 1987), p. 43.
6. Chester G. Starr, *A History of the Ancient World* (New York: Oxford Univ. Press, 1983), p. 82.
7. William Hardy McNeill, *A World History* (New York: Oxford Univ. Press, 1967), p. 43.
8. Immanuel Velikovsky, *Ages in Chaos* (New York: Doubleday & Co., 1952), pp. 56-57.
9. "*The Admonitions of Ipu-Wer*", translated by John A. Wilson, ni *Ancient Near Eastern Texts*, ed. James B. Pritchard (New Jersey: Princeton Univ. Press, 1969), pp.441-42.
10. S.N. Kramer, *The Sumerians* (Chicago: 1963), p.142.
11. E. Hawkridge, *Indian Gods and Kings* (1964), p.10.
12. H.G. Rawlinson, *India, A Short Cultural History*, p.18.
13. Elijah Muhammad, *Message to the Blackman in America* (Chicago: Muhammad's Temple No. 2, 1965), pp. 110-121.
14. *New Encyclopaedia Britannica*, 1979, s.v. "Troy."
15. Georges Augustin Barrois,"*Chronology, Metrology, Etc.,*" in

The Interpreter's Bible, vol. I, ed. Nolan B. Harmon (New York: Abingdon-Cokesbury Press, 1952), pp.142-45. Also, Alexander Winchell, Preadamites (Chicago: S.C. Griggs & Co., 1880).

16. Elijah Muhammad, *Message to the Blackman in America* (Chicago: Muhammad's Temple No. 2, 1965), pp. 94-95,121, 133.
17. James George Frazer, *Folk-Lore in the Old Testament* (New York: Macmillan Co., 1923), pp. 11-12.
18. *Account of the Island of Ceylon*, John Davy, cited by Alexander Winchell, *Preadamites* (Chicago:1880), pp.349-350.
19. L.Bolk, *"Origin of Racial Characteristics in Man,"* in *American Journal of Physical Anthropology* (New York: A.R. Liss) 31:1., quoted by H.P.Wassermann, *Ethnic Pigmentation*: Historical, *Physiological and Clinical Aspects* (New York: American Elsevier Publ., 1974), p.58.
20. Charles Darwin, *"The Races of Man,"* in *The Descent of Man and Selection in Relation to Sex*, vol.1 (London: Murray, 1871), pp.248-49.
21. Charles Darwin, *"The Races of Man,"* in *The Descent of Man and Selection in Relation to Sex* (London: D. Appleton & Co., 1915), pp. 184-85.
22. James C. Pritchard, *Researches into the Physical History of Man*, ed. George W. Stocking (Chicago: Univ. of Chicago Press), p.lv.
23. Edwin Grant Conklin, *"The Trend of Evolution,"* in *The Evolution of Man*, ed. George Alfred Baitsell (New Haven: Yale Univ. Press, 1922), p.174.
24. Bernard Ramm, *The Christian View of Science and the Scripture* (Michigan: Eerdmans Publ., 1968), p. 339.
25. *Midrash Rabbah*, vol.5, translated by H. Freedman (New York: Soncino Press, 1983), pp. 308-309.
26. Robert Eisler, "*Metallurgical Anthropology in Hesiod and Plato*," in *Isis: An International Review Devoted to the*

History of Science and Civilization, vol. 40, No. 120, (Philadelphia: Univ. of Penn., 1949), p.110.

27. Hesiod, *Works and Days*, quoted in, John Mansley Robinson, *An Introduction to Early Greek Philosophy* (Boston: Houghton Mifflin, 1968), pp. 12-12.
28. Riane Eisler, The Chalice and the Blade (San Francisco: Harper & Row, 1987), p.63.
29. Riane Eisler, The Chalice and the Blade (San Francisco: Harper & Row, 1987), p.64.
30. Shah-Nama, in *The Sacred Books and Early Literature of the East*, vol. VII, (New York: Parke, Austin, and Lipscomb), p. 294.
31. *The Epic of the Kings: Shah-Nama, the National Epic of Persia, by Ferdowsi*, translated by Reuben Levy, ed. E. Yar-Shater,(Chicago: Univ. of Chicago Press, 1967), p. 36.
32. *Book of Enoch*, translated by Richard Laurence (Calif: Artisan Sales, 1980), p.92.
33. *Book of Enoch*, translated by Richard Laurence (Calif: Artisan Sales, 1980), pp.92-93.
34. *Book of Enoch*, translated by Richard Laurence (Calif: Artisan Sales, 1980), p.93.
35. *The Holy Qur'an*, 2:28, translated by Maulana Muhammad Ali (Lahore: Ahmadiyya Anjuman Isha'at Islam, 1985).
36. C.W. Shields, *The Scientific Evidences of Revealed Religion* (New York: Scribner, 1900), p. 124, cited by Bernard Ramm, *The Christian View of Science and Scripture* (Michigan: Eerdmans Publ., 1968), p.321.
37. Reginald Stuart Poole, *Genesis of the Earth and of Man*, cited by The Duke of Argyll, *Primeval Man* (New York: John B. Alden, 1884), p. 35., see also Alexander Winchell, *Preadamites* (Chicago: 1880), p. 463.
38. *J.P. Thompson, Man in Genesis and Geology* (New York: 1875), pp. 106-107.
39. Marcelino Mendez y Pelayo, *Historia de los Heterodoxos Espanoles*, vol. VII (Buenos Aries: Libreria Perlado, 1945),

pp. 324-325.
40. Leon Poliakov, *The Aryan Myth*, translated by Edmund Howard (New York: Basic Books, 1971), p. 131.
41. Arno Borst, *Der Turmbau von Babel*, vol. I,(Stuttgart: 1957), p. 339.
42. Arno Borst, *Der Turmbau von Babel*, vol. I,(Stuttgart: 1957), p. 358. see also, *The Holy Qur'an*, 2:28.
43. Isaac de La Peyrere, *Men Before Adam*, (London: 1656), p. 56.
44. "*Book of Romans*", 5:12-14, in *The Holy Bible: Commonly Known as the Authorized (King James) Version.*
45. A.T. White, *Men Before Adam* (New York: Random House), p.58.
46. Manahem M. Kasher, *Encyclopedia of Biblical Interpretation*, vol. 1, translated by Harry Freedman (New York: Amer. Biblical Encyclo. Society), p.59.
47. "*Book of Genesis*", 1:27 and 5:2, in *The Holy Bible: Commonly Known as the Authorized (King James) Version.*
48. "*Book of Genesis*", 1:26, in *The Holy Bible: Commonly Known as the Authorized (King James) Version.*
49. J.D. Douglas, *The New Bible Dictionary*, s.v. "God" (Grand Rapids: Eerdmans, 1962), pp. 474-75. see also *The Broadman Bible Commentary*, vol. 1, ed. Clifton J. Allen, (Nashville: Broadman Press, 1969), p. 122.
50. G. de Purucker, *Fundamentals of the Esoteric Philosophy*, (Pasadena: Theosophical Univ. Press, 1979), p. 99. see also, Robert D. Sacks, *A Commentary on the Book of Genesis*, (1990), p. 15.
51. *The International Standard Bible Encyclopaedia*, vol. 2, ed. James Orr, s.v. "God" (Michigan: Eerdmans Publ.,1939), p. 1254.
52. "*Book of Exodus*", 7:1, in *The Holy Bible: Commonly Known as the Authorized (King James) Version.*
53. *The International Standard Bible Encyclopaedia*, vol. 2, ed. James Orr, s.v. "God" (Michigan: Eerdmans Publ.,1939),

p. 1254.

54. R.A. Finlayson, *The New Bible Dictionary*, ed. J.D. Douglas, s.v. "God" (Grand Rapids: Eerdmans Publ., 1982), p.474.
55. *Encyclopaedia of Religion and Ethics*, vol. 1, ed. James Hastings (New York: Scribner, 1913), p. 84.
56. *The American College Dictionary*, ed. C.L. Barnhart, s.v. "ruddy" (New York: Random House, 1970), p.1056.
57. H.P. Wassermann, *Ethnic Pigmentation: Historical, Physiological and Clinical Aspects* (New York: American Elsevier Publ. 1974), p. 15. see also R.D. Simons, *The Colour of the Skin in Human Relations* (Amsterdam: Elsevier Publ., 1961).
58. *Preadamites*, Alexander Winchell (Chicago: 1880), p.161.
59. William Gesenius, *A Hebrew and English Lexicon*, translated by Edward Robinson (Boston: Crocker & Brewster, 1854), p.414.
60. Elijah Muhammad, *Message to the Blackman in America* (Chicago: Muhammad's Temple No. 2, 1965), pp. 117-18.
61. Elijah Muhammad, *Message to the Blackman in America* (Chicago: Muhammad's Temple No. 2, 1965), p. 103.
62. Elijah Muhammad, *Message to the Blackman in America* (Chicago: Muhammad's Temple No. 2, 1965), p. 116.
63. Elijah Muhammad, *Message to the Blackman in America* (Chicago: Muhammad's Temple No. 2, 1965), p. 117.
64. Elijah Muhammad, *Message to the Blackman in America* (Chicago: Muhammad's Temple No. 2, 1965), p. 117.
65. Elijah Muhammad, *Message to the Blackman in America* (Chicago: Muhammad's Temple No. 2, 1965), pp. 117-18
66. Elijah Muhammad, *Message to the Blackman in America* (Chicago: Muhammad's Temple No. 2, 1965), p. 103.
67. Diodorus, "*Book XL,*" in *Diodorus of Sicily*, vol.XII, translated by Francis R. Walton (Cambridge: Harvard Univ. Press, 1977), p.281.
68. Diodorus, "*Book XXXIV,*" in *Diodorus of Sicily*, vol.XII, translated by Francis R. Walton (Cambridge: Harvard Univ.

Press, 1977), p.53.
69. *Encyclopaedia Judaica*, vol. 3., s.v. "azazel" (New York: Macmillan & Co., 1971), p.1002.
70. *The American College Dictionary*, ed. by C.L. Barnhart, s.v. "pestilent" (New York: Random House, 1970), p.906.
71. "*The First Book of Adam and Eve,*" in *The Lost Books of the Bible and The Forgotten Books of Eden* (Collins Publ., 1963), p. 3.
72. "*The First Book of Adam and Eve,*" in *The Lost Books of the Bible and The Forgotten Books of Eden*, (Collins Publ., 1963), p. 5.
73. "*The First Book of Adam and Eve,*" in *The Lost Books of the Bible and The Forgotten Books of Eden* (Collins Publ., 1963), p. 6.
74. "*The First Book of Adam and Eve,*" in *The Lost Books of the Bible and The Forgotten Books of Eden* (Collins Publ., 1963), p. 7.
75. Bashir Ahmed Dar, *Religious Thought of Sayyid Ahmed Khan* (Lahore: Institute of Islamic Culture, 1957), pp. 242-43.
76. *The Encyclopaedia of Islam, New Edition*, ed. B. Lewis, s.v. "Iblis" (London: Luzac & Co., 1971), p. 669.
77. M.J. Kister, "*Legends in Tafsir and Hadith Literature: The Creation of Adam and Related Stories,*" in *Approaches to the History of the Qur'an*, ed. Adrew Rippin (Oxford: Clarendon Press, 1988), p.89.
78. E.J. Brill's First Encyclopaedia of Islam, ed. A.J. Wensinck, s.v. "Iblis" (New York: E.J. Brill, 1987), p. 351.
79. Stephen H. Langdon, "*The Devils, Demons, Good and Evil Spirits,*" in *The Mythology of All Races*, ed. John MacCulloch(Boston: Marshall Jones Co., 1931), p.352.
80. George Roe, Iblis in Paradise: A Story of the Temptation (Philadelphia: Henry Altemus Co., 1908), unnumbered pages.
81. B. Allen Donaldson, *The Wild Rue: A Study of Muhammadan Magic and Folklore in Iran* (London: Luzac & Co., 1938), p. 354.

82. Essad-Bey, *Twelve Secrets of the Caucasus*, translated by G. Chychele Waterston (New York: Viking Press,1931) p.310.
83. *The Holy Qur'an*, translated by Maulawi Sher Ali (Pakistan: Oriental and Religious Publ., 1979), p. 638.
84. Margaret Kahn, *Children of the Jinn: In Search of the Kurds and their Country*, (New York: Seaview Books, 1980), p.xi.
85. S. Hoogasian-Villa, *100 Armenian Tales, and their Folkloristic Relevance*, p.30.
86. Elijah Muhammad, *Message to the Blackman in America* (Chicago: Muhammad's Temple No. 2, 1965), p. 125.
87. "*Book of Leviticus*," 16:21, 22, in *The Holy Bible: Commonly Known as the Authorized (King James) Version*.
88. *Encyclopaedia Judaica*, vol. 3, s.v. "azazel" (New York: Macmillan & Co.,1971), p.1002.
89. *Encyclopaedia Judaica*, vol. 3, s.v."azazel" (New York: Macmillan & Co.,1971), p.999.
90. James George Frazer, "*The Scapegoat*," in *The Golden Bough*, part 6, (New York: Macmillan, 1951), p. 210.
91. *Book of Enoch*, translated by Richard Laurence (Calif: Artisan Sales, 1980), pp. 3-4.
92. *"Book of Enoch,"* translated by M.A. Knibb in *The Apocryphal Old Testament*, ed. H.F.D. Sparks (Oxford: Clarendon Press, 1984), pp. 195-96.
93. *The American College Dictionary*, ed. C.L. Barnhart, s.v. "generation", (New York: Random House, 1970), p.505.
94. James George Frazer, "*The Scapegoat*," in *The Golden Bough*, part 6, (New York: Macmillan, 1951), pp. 219-221.
95. Elijah Muhammad, *Message to the Blackman in America* (Chicago: Muhammad's Temple No. 2, 1965), pp. 117-18.
96. Pliny, *Natural History*, vol. II, book VI, translated by H. Rackham (Cambridge: Harvard Univ. Press, 1938), p.359.
97. H.N. Wethered, *The Mind of the Ancient World* (New York: Longmans, Green & Co., 1937), p.270.
98. H.N. Wethered, *The Mind of the Ancient World*, p.270.
99. Anonymous, *Tagebuch*, pp.33-34. cited by John F. Baddeley,

The Rugged Flanks of Caucasus, vol. 1 (London: Oxford Univ. Press, 1940), p. 155.

100. John F. Baddeley, *The Rugged Flanks of Caucasus*, vol. 2 (London: Oxford Univ. Press, 1940), p.62.
101. John F. Baddeley, The Rugged Flanks of Caucasus, vol. 1 (London: Oxford Univ. Press, 1940), p.156.
102. William Hardy McNeill, *A World History* (New York: Oxford Univ. Press, 1967), p.113.
103. *Ancient Near Eastern Texts*, ed. James B. Pritchard (New Jersey: Princeton Univ. Press, 1969), p. 442.
104. *Lewis Spence, Myths and Legends of Babylonia and Assyria* (London: George G. Harrap & Co., 1916), pp. 89-90.
105. *Lewis Spence, Myths and Legends of Babylonia and Assyria* (London: George G. Harrap & Co., 1916), p. 35.
106. Arnold Heeren, *Historical Researches into the Politics, Intercourse and Trade of the Carthaginians, Ethiopians and Egyptians*, vol. 1 (Oxford: D.A. Talboys, 1832), p.86.
107. Arnold Heeren, *Historical Researches into the Politics, Intercourse and Trade of the Carthaginians, Ethiopians and Egyptians*, vol. 1 (Oxford: D.A. Talboys, 1832), p.86.
108. Manetho, *"Aegyptiaca," translated by W.G. Waddell* (Cambridge: Harvard Univ. Press 1940), p. 83.
109. Essad-Bey, *Twelve Secrets of the Caucasus*, translated by G. Chychele Waterston (New York: Viking Press, 1931), p. 128.
110. Essad-Bey, *Twelve Secrets of the Caucasus*, translated by G. Chychele Waterston (New York: Viking Press, 1931), p. 311.
111. Essad-Bey, *Twelve Secrets of the Caucasus*, translated by G. Chychele Waterston (New York: Viking Press, 1931), p. 312.
112. John F. Baddeley, The Rugged Flanks of Caucasus, vol.2 (London: Oxford Univ. Press, 1940), p.236.
113. Mardiros A. Ananikian "*Armenian Mythology,*" in *The Mythology of All Races*, ed. John MacCulloch (Boston: Marshall Jones Co., 1931), pp.98-99.
114. John F. Baddeley, *The Rugged Flanks of Caucasus,* vol.2 (London: Oxford Univ. Press, 1940), p.234.

115. Elijah Muhammad, *Message to the Blackman in America* (Chicago: Muhammad's Temple No. 2, 1965), pp. 119-20.
116. John F. Baddeley, *The Rugged Flanks of Caucasus*, vol.1 (London: Oxford Univ. Press, 1940), p.156.
117. W. Boyd Dawkins, *Cave Hunting, Researches on the Evidence of Caves, Respecting the Early Inhabitants of Europe* (London: MacMillan & Co., 1874), pp.102-103.
118. *The Holy Qu'ran*, 18:17-18, translated by Maulana Muhammad Ali (Lahore: Ahmadiyya Anjuman Isha'at Islam, 1985).
119. *O. Schrader, Prehistoric Antiquities of the Aryan Peoples*, translated by Frank Byron Jfvons (London: Griffin & Co., 1890), pp.340-41.
120. Tacitus, *Germania*, translated by H. Mattingly (New York: Penguin Books, 1970) p.115
121. Xenophon Anabasis, *Books IV-VII*, translated by Carlton L. Brown (London: Harvard Univ. Press, 1922), pp. 110-111.
122. *O. Schrader, Prehistoric Antiquities of the Aryan Peoples*, translated by Frank Byron Jfvons (London: Griffin & Co., 1890), pp.340-41.
123. Elijah Muhammad, *Message to the Blackman in America* (Chicago: Muhammad's Temple No. 2, 1965), p. 103.
124. *Jamasp-Namak*, vol. 2, translated by Darmester, cited by Louis H. Gray, *Encyclopaedia of Religion and Ethics*, (1925), p.507.
125. *Dinkard*, book IX, chapter XXI, verse XIX, in *Sacred Books of the East Series: Pahlavi Texts*, part IV, translated by E.W. West, ed. F. Max Muller (Delhi: Motilal Banarsidass, 1965), pp. 216-17.
126. M.N. Dhalla, *Zoroastrian Theology* (New York: 1914), pp. 8,160.
127. A.G. Warner, *Shah Nama*, cited in *Encyclopaedia of Religion and Ethics*, ed. James Hastings, s.v. "Mazandaran" (New York: Scribner, 1927), p.507.
128. B. Allen Donaldson, The Wild Rue: A Study of

Muhammadan Magic and Folklore in Iran (London: Luzac & Co., 1938), p.43.
129. Verrier Elwin, Tribal Myths of Orissa (London: Oxford Univ. Press, 1954), p.442.
130. *Shah-Nama*, in *The Sacred Books and Early Literature of the East*, vol. VII (New York: Parke, Austin, and Lipscomb), p. 317.
131. *Shah-Nama*, in *The Sacred Books and Early Literature of the East*, vol. VII (New York: Parke, Austin, and Lipscomb), p. 317.
132. Diodorus, *Book I*,88, ed. C.H. Oldfather (Cambridge: Harvard Univ. Press, 1933).
133. *The Sky-Religion in Egypt*, G.A. Wainwright (London: Cambridge Univ. Press, 1938), p.31. see *Hieratic Papyri in the British Museum* (Third Series), I, Text, pp. 10, 20, 21.
134. G.A. Wainwright, *The Sky-Religion in Egypt: Its Antiquity and Effects*, (London: Cambridge Univ. Press, 1938), pp.44-45.
135. Plutarch, *De Iside et Osiride*, Sec.73 (Cardiff: Univ. of Wales, 1970).
136. Diodorus, *Book I*,88., ed. C.H. Oldfather (Cambridge: Harvard Univ. Press, 1933).
137. The Sky-Religion in Egypt, G.A. Wainwright (London:Cambridge Univ. Press, 1938), pp. 31-32.
138. Elijah Muhammad, *Message to the Blackman in America* (Chicago: Muhammad's Temple No. 2, 1965), p. 120.
139. Chester G. Starr, *A History of the Ancient World* (New York: Oxford Univ. Press, 1983), p. 82.
140. Elijah Muhammad, *Message to the Blackman in America* (Chicago: Muhammad's Temple No. 2, 1965), pp. 93, 120.
141. Hendrik Willem van Loon, *The Story of Mankind* (Liveright Publ., 1962), p. 17.
142. Diodorus, *Book I*,88. ed., C.H. Oldfather (Cambridge: Harvard Univ. Press, 1933)
143. Manetho, quoted by Josephus in *Against Apion*, translated by

H. St. J. Thackeray (Cambridge: Harvard Univ. Press, 1966), p.265.

144. Elijah Muhammad, *Message to the Blackman in America* (Chicago: Muhammad's Temple No. 2, 1965), p. 104.